Staying Power

Surviving Ministry Long Term

Wayne Peat

Staying Power: Surviving Ministry Long Term

Softcover ISBN 978-0-473-26330-0

Kindle ISBN 978-0-473-26331-7

First Printing

This book is dedicated to my wife Wendy

who stood with me, and whose love, grace and faithfulness,

God used to help sustain me

through the massive highs and the devastating lows

of our incredible ministry leadership journey.

Contents

Testimonials

"Wayne Peat addresses many of the underlying reasons for the endemic failure evident in ministry today. Whether that failure comes from insecurity in identity, the unexpected emotional demands of ministry, the performance trap or from unrealistic expectations, each area is identified, analyzed and ways of either avoiding or recovering from the pitfalls are discussed. The material is based on a course that Wayne designed and taught at our Bible College. It was rated as one of the most relevant courses taken, by our second-year ministry interns.

"It is a powerful book, that I am sure will be of enormous value to both the new minister and the seasoned veteran."

Shane Bermingham, BMS (Hons) C.M.A., B.Div
Principal
Ministry Training College of New Zealand

"Christian ministry is tough. My pastor and friend Wayne Peat has gone the distance, enduring and persevering through the mountains and the valleys, and he has acquired a great deal of wisdom to share. This book will be of tremendous service to the body of Christ at large, and particularly to those who are called of God to serve in the ministry. I unreservedly commend the book, and the author, to you."

Steve Burgess
Senior Pastor
C3 Church Christchurch, NZ

"In his book *Staying Power*, Wayne brings a wealth of experience as a Pastor and Leader in the churches he has ministered in and has oversight of. Having a deep sense of identity and security in Jesus Christ, rather than the various forms of church success measures, is key to longevity in ministry and Christian service. Wayne underlines the importance of this and on the essential, ongoing and deepening relationship with Christ to give those in God's service, the vision and strength to persevere towards fruitfulness.

"The statistics concerning those leaving the ministry are alarming. *Staying Power* therefore addresses the key elements to assist 'staying' rather than 'leaving' in ten easy to read chapters.

"*Staying Power* is a 'must read' for anyone either seriously contemplating ministry, in training or currently in church leadership. Wayne's Spirit inspired insight and sound theological astuteness makes this book an essential addition to any library."

Andrew Wood
Director, Howick Counselling
B.Sc. M.Ed. Admin (Hons) M.A. (Couns) P.G. Dip Ed (Couns)

Acknowledgements

I am so deeply appreciative for the "beautiful field" that I now find myself in for the final chapter of my ministry. Over the last decade in the C3 Church Global Movement with the inspiring leadership of founders Pastor Phil and Chris Pringle, and C3 Pacific Regional Directors Pastors Dean and Fiona Rush, I have learned more about myself and "the doing of church" than in all the previous two decades of ministry.

I am forever grateful for the faith, grace and authenticity which are the intrinsic qualities of C3. In this place of enthusiasm, encouragement and equipping from passionate but wise and godly leaders, I have been motivated, grown and stretched to reach more of my dreams for the building of Christ's kingdom, than I thought might have been possible.

I am thankful, too, to all of the pastors in the C3 Pacific Region, whose friendship and comradeship in ministry are a priceless treasure.

Thank you also to Naomi Rogers who took on the task of the preliminary editing, to Loretta Crum (ebooksalon.net) for the final editing of this book for me, and to my daughter-in-law Shayna Peat for adding the family touch with her cover design.

– ***Wayne Peat***

Foreword

To succeed as a leader, one of the most fundamental issues is the ability to go the distance. You can have all the gifts and talents in the world. But if you can't stand up under pressure and keep moving forward, you will not live at your full potential.

In my role of developing leaders I have seen some very gifted and talented people stumble at the hurdles along the way and ultimately give up. It is always a sad sight. So many leaders today want it all and want it now, with not enough thought to building character and endurance into their lives. If only they could stay in the game and see their potential become success.

Wayne Peat has been in ministry for thirty-one years and has pastored three churches. I have worked with him closely for the last eight years in the areas of church planting and leadership coaching. He has demonstrated this quality of endurance and faithfulness and has the authority to speak on the subject. This book will help you to navigate the twists and turns of leadership and inspire you and practically help you to make it. The ability to develop staying power is one of the most crucial topics for any leader or aspiring leader.

Pastor Dean Rush
Regional Director
C3 Pacific

Introduction

This book is written for anyone who is contemplating or who has already embarked on the adventurous and tremendous journey of ministry leadership. It is especially written to help pastors and other ministry leaders go the distance. The attrition rate for pastors is extraordinarily high. One study by Duke University found that eighty-five percent of Bible college graduates entering ministry leave within five years. Ninety percent of all pastors will not remain until retirement. Another study by the Fuller Seminary suggests fifty percent of pastors drop out of ministry within the first five years. Many never return to church.[1]

These statistics make for sobering reading. Clearly the role of ministry leadership is incredibly testing. The causes for such a high dropout rate are varied and complex. It is easy to see that a high degree of resilience is required. This book seeks to examine some of the main areas of vulnerability that cause the ministry leader to stumble or give up and discusses ways to overcome them.

I remember well my own start in pastoral ministry. After several years as a volunteer at various levels including leadership in the church, God opened up a wide door of ministry opportunity. I was invited to serve as an assistant to the pastor of a Baptist Church in a provincial town. This offer was the realization of a dream I had carried for a while. The sense of "call" had been ignited not long after my conversion to Christ. I had enthusiastically waited for the day of release, while preparing theologically and serving in my church on the back of a busy career and a young family. Finally it had come.

It came suddenly, just as I was beginning to feel that I might not have heard God correctly. That day while walking in the park on my lunch break I had prayed, "Lord, I believe that you want me to serve in pastoral ministry but I will serve you in business if that is what you want. I will do whatever you want." A great peace filled me. At the exact moment I returned to my office there was a phone call. It was from a leader of the denomination I was in. The caller said, "Wayne, I'm just calling to encourage you. I believe God is going to open a ministry door for you soon!" Then he just hung up! It was very uncanny and felt kind of random. When I arrived home that night and pulled into the driveway, Wendy called out: "Wayne, phone for you!" It was the church, inquiring about my availability. I love it when God answers prayer that quickly!

A few weeks later, and still yet to make a firm decision, I visited a church lead by Pastor David McCracken, an anointed prophetic minister. That day I received a prophetic word which I still have, written out and filed away. All these years later I am impressed by its specific application. Consider these extracts from what David sensed God was to saying to me at that important moment.

"It is a time when I would open other doors for you. It is a time when I would cause your pathway to change. It is the time when I would cause your eyes to be opened to the harvest…it is a time for fresh decision and challenge…it is the hour that I have groomed you for." There is more but you get the picture. It was the time!

At the end of the prophetic word, David described this picture. In hindsight, it is a poignant reminder to me that God has his plans worked out for us.

"I see a large field full of good things. It is not a bad field, in fact I see a large field full of good things, beautiful grass growing in it. It is a beautiful place. Then I see a little narrow path which shoots off at a tangent and it doesn't look like that beautiful field that you are standing in. I see the hand of God tugging you in your spirit and as you take that path it takes you out of that beautiful field. You are kind of looking back over your shoulder thinking 'Am I crazy?' As you are walking down that narrow dusty path suddenly you break through to the other side. There – is a field which is twice as large and twice as beautiful but you couldn't see it. You couldn't see it until you took the steps of obedience that God has spoken to your spirit."

As cryptic as prophetic words can be until the Holy Spirit brings revelation, this word proved to be a succinct metaphorical map of my future ministry pathway. As I reflect, it is exactly how things have been. My ministry journey has been divided into three parts. It started in a large and beautiful field, digressed into the narrow and dusty path, then by God's unfathomable grace, led into the field twice as large and twice as beautiful as the first.

When reading over the prophecy, I always skipped over the narrow, dusty path bit. Besides it was just a few words sandwiched between more appealing promises. Beautiful fields are good places to be in. Dusty paths are not. God had blessed me greatly in my early years of ministry. The ministries I led grew rapidly. They were heady days but God knew that if he was to bless me further, there were some things in me that needed to be sorted out. I didn't know it when the moment came, but I did step out of that first beautiful field and began to walk that narrow path.

That interlude turned out to be my wilderness. The Spirit had led me there to be tested. I cannot say I passed the test. I can only say that while I did not prove faithful, God remained faithful, and eventually brought me through to the other side. That time was one of the darkest periods of my life. Both marriage and ministry were almost sacrificed on the altar of pride. That pride masked a deep insecurity which subconsciously polluted my ministry motives. That dry pathway was littered with the stumbling stones of perceived failure, real failure, accumulated hurts, frustration, depression and despair. It knocked me down and out for the count.

Now, before you put this book down fearing it might discourage rather than encourage you, allow me to reiterate. This is written from the place of victory, not defeat. I am now in that "twice as beautiful" field. God enabled me to rise again when I thought I could not. I want to encourage you, no matter what you may face in the rigors of your ministry journey. It is in the darkest hours that light shines brightest. It is our God who is able to bring forth the *"treasures hidden in the darkness"* (Isaiah 45:3).

It was in that place that God revealed my weaknesses. He also showed me the greatness of his love, grace and power. The hard-won lessons learned then (and since) I desire to pass on to you, the ministry leader. I have found that it is the emotional demands of ministry that cause a ministry leader to come unstuck.

The power of the emotional challenges in ministry to destroy are directly related to issues of the heart. No Bible college will adequately teach you or prepare you fully for what you may face in this area. You will likely have to go through your own learning experiences. However, the aim of this book is to make you aware of, if not help you avoid altogether, the many pitfalls that can take you out. I don't want you to be naïve.

To serve God in a ministry leadership capacity is a glorious privilege, but as Pastor Phil Pringle says, "The anointing does not come without cost." I humbly pass on to you what I have discovered to be the keys to "staying power" so that you will be a ministry leader who remains for the long haul.

End Note:

[1]Bryan Fulthorp, www.bluechippastor.org/2013/05/04 on the attrition rate of pastors

Chapter One
Having a Strong Sense of Call

Every Christian is called by God. The call of God is the hearing of God's voice. To hear that call, and to embrace it, is the essence of fullness of life. Wherever God places you, his call is the powerful internal driver that fills your thoughts and actions with meaning and purpose. Having clarity and conviction around your call is vital, especially when that call is to church ministry leadership. Without a strong sense of call, you will not survive the glorious but rigorous journey the call entails. You must know that God is at work, in the work that you do.

As I climbed the steps of the baptismal pool feeling the intense love and presence of God, I heard the words of my friend: "Here comes three years of Bible college coming up!" This was the first sowing of the seed. God nurtured it to become a compelling call to serve in leadership in his church.

Ahead were the challenging years of being "made ready," but even those times did not fully prepare me for what was to come. I began full time ministry as a new and naïve soldier, proud of the badge and uniform, eager for the adventure and the glory of battles to be won for Jesus. I soon discovered, however, that church leadership was not an easy ride. Instead it was the front line of the cosmic conflict. There, the fight is intensely ferocious. There, all the forces of the enemy have one goal. That is to knock you, the leader, out!

Before you are disheartened, I say to you now as a seasoned campaigner of over thirty years in ministry leadership that I still love what I do. Yes, there have been many battles and many losses. The victories, though, have been far more frequent, greater and sweeter. One thing only has anchored me to the task: the call of God. The call apprehends you. It sustains you, especially in the heat of the battle. That is why the call must be strong in your heart.

There have been many times when I have wanted to give up, when I have thought, "I would rather be doing something else!" But because of the power of God's call, I know that bottom line; there is nothing else I would rather be doing.

Despite the challenges, there is nothing more meaningful than doing that which you have been made for. There is an indefinable joy that comes when you have found your niche. To know God's call with certainty to a particular course, whatever that may be, brings with it the innate desire and resilience to fulfill it.

Paying the cost

Receiving God's call to ministry leadership brings wonderful blessing when it is embraced in obedience and full surrender to his grace and empowerment. Yet, the pursuit of the call of God does not come without considerable cost.

The challenge comes at the first step after the moment of call is realized. There is always something that needs to be laid down. To be required to pay the price from the beginning is an essential test of God's call. Many who aspire to ministry leadership default at this point. They are unwilling to give up a job, a good income, a home, or some other idol in which their security rests. I know of many called by God to ministry leadership who are instead locked into lifestyles which keep them caged in unfulfilled desire and discontent. If the cost seems too high at the outset, there is no chance that the on-going cost of the journey will be sustained. It has to be this way.

Jesus Christ, is our primary model for church leadership. He said, *"I am the good shepherd. The good shepherd lays his life down for the sheep"* (John 10:11). This analogy highlights the nature of the responsibility of the leader to those entrusted into his care. It emphasizes the ongoing cost associated with the call. The chances are that you will not literally give your life to die as Jesus did. But the implications are clear; you will be required (at least metaphorically) to lay down your own interests in many ways.

Jesus never does a "sell" job when he calls. To enter ministry leadership with a glamour view of an ultimate high visibility platform ministry, a large church and the accolades of men will inevitably bring disillusionment and failure. Ministry leadership is never meant to be about self-serving.

Jesus was extremely candid about the sacrifices intrinsic to ministry. He warned of those who would lead with self-centered motives. Such a person is *"a hired hand"* who *"will run when he sees the wolf coming,"* (John 10:13) without concern for those he is responsible for. If you are in it for yourself, this will be revealed. When the pressure comes, you will inevitably bail. The hired hand only carries the responsibility if it profits him. The good shepherd remains so long as it profits those entrusted to his care. Jesus said, *"Wherever your treasure is, there your heart and thoughts will be"*

(Matthew 6:21). Ultimately, how much you value the call and those you serve is reflected in the price you are willing to pay for it.

In his great cause, be aware that there will be times when the forces of hell will come against you. If you are called to ministry leadership, never embrace the call of God with some sort of glossy view of the charge set before you. You are called to fight against an enemy whose purpose is to rob you of God's blessings. Remember, though, with God's power and authority on you, *"No weapon turned against you will succeed"* (Isaiah 54:17). Be assured that your serving will know its unfathomable rewards in this life and the next. God's word tells us that nothing compares with what he has to gift to his own, who serve him faithfully.

Am I really called?

A wrong motive in pursuing the call is one thing. Not being certain of the call is another. To doubt the call is an important factor that undermines resilience in ministry.

In fulfilling the call of God there will be times when you are confronted with unexpected challenges and disappointments. There will be countless moments when you will feel like the wheels are coming off. There will be times when you will feel discouraged, disillusioned and frustrated. Opposition, criticism, heartache and failures are the inevitable experiences of ministry leadership. Every ministry leader will face periods of extreme and diverse pressures. Your readiness to face up to and overcome that pressure matters. In those times you may find yourself questioning the validity of the call: "Did I hear God correctly? Am I where I should be?" This is completely normal.

When your whole being is screaming at you to give up, it will be your ability to affirm the call that holds you to the task. For this reason it is important to be clear and certain in your own mind that God has called you.

Feelings alone tend to be unreliable when the call is challenged. It is helpful to carry out an objective assessment of the specific ways and events that shaped your call.

It is important that you are able to reflect on the particular evidences that occurred over the time the call was given to you. If you can do this, it helps to reinforce the call, enabling you to be resolute in staying the course.

The ways God calls his leaders

A call cannot be described in any one way, but those who have heard from God recognize the constraint it contains. So long as the heart is inclined towards obedience, you cannot do anything else. God calls each of us in a unique and powerful fashion. While some patterns may be repeated, the circumstances of each person's call differ. You will have your own special story, resonating and settling into the deepest recesses of your spirit. The following Biblical examples illustrate some of the ways in which God calls his leaders.

Moses (called by God through an angel in a burning bush)

One day Moses was tending the flock of his father-in-law, Jethro, the priest of Midian, and he went deep into the wilderness near Sinai, the mountain of God. Suddenly, the angel of the lord appeared to him in a blazing fire in a bush. Moses was amazed because the bush was engulfed in flames, but it didn't burn up. "Amazing!" Moses said to himself. "Why isn't that bush burning up? I must go over to see this." When the Lord saw he had caught Moses attention, ***God called to him from the bush,*** *"Moses! Moses!* (Exodus 3:1-4)

Samuel (called by the audible voice of God)

Samuel did not yet know the Lord because he had never had a message from the Lord before. So now the Lord called a third time, and once more Samuel jumped up and ran to Eli. "Here I am," he said "What do you need?" Then Eli realized it was the Lord who was calling the boy. So he said to Samuel, "Go and lie down again, and if someone calls again, say 'Yes Lord, your servant is listening.' So Samuel went back to bed. ***And the Lord came and called as before, "Samuel! Samuel!"*** (1 Samuel 3:7-10)

David (called by God through the prophet Samuel)

And ***the Lord said "This is the one, anoint him."*** *So as David stood there among his brothers, Samuel took the olive oil he had brought and poured it on David's head. And the Spirit of the Lord came mightily upon him from that day on. (1 Samuel 16:13)*

The Apostles: Peter, Andrew, James and John (called by God through the person of Jesus)

One day as Jesus was walking along the shore beside the sea of Galilee, he saw two brothers – Simon, also called Peter, and Andrew, fishing with a net, for they were commercial fishermen. Jesus called out to them, " ***"Come, be my disciples,*** *and I will show you how to fish for people!" So they left their nets at once and went and followed him.* (Matthew 4:18-20)

Paul (called by God through a supernatural visitation of Jesus)

As he was nearing Damascus...***a brilliant light from heaven suddenly beamed down upon him! He fell to the ground and heard a voice saying to him,*** *"Saul, Saul! Why are you persecuting me?" "Who are you, sir?" Paul asked. And the voice replied, "I am Jesus, the one you are persecuting! Now get up and go into the city, and* ***you will be told what you are to do."*** (Acts 9:3-5)

Timothy (called by God through the ministry of Paul)

"Timothy, my son, ***here are my instructions based on the prophetic words spoken*** *about you earlier."* (1 Timothy 1:18)

"This is why I remind you to fan into flames ***the spiritual gift God gave you when I laid my hands on you."*** *(*2 Timothy 1:6)

From the above examples we see that the call of God may come through supernatural circumstances and events and by natural means. God may call you through a "burning bush" experience, dreams, open visions, a prophetic word, the written Word of God or the encouragement and direction of other godly servants. He may use one or several of these ways. In the tough times, being able to review the ways in which God shaped your call will give you reassurance you are where God wants you to be.

I remember clearly a prophetic word and picture given when I had asked for prayer from others for God's direction in the early stages of my own call to ministry. A very godly, elderly woman in a home group I attended saw a picture of buildings like school classrooms and an area with children's play equipment. This, she felt, was the context in which the Lord would ultimately place me. To be honest, I thought, "She's got that wrong! I don't want to be a school teacher!" In my mind the vision had no bearing on what God was calling me to do. I promptly dismissed it and forgot about it. You can imagine my surprise when some years later, on my first day at the church where I had been called to serve, I looked out of my office window and saw classrooms and a children's playground used by the Sunday school. The long forgotten prophetic word and picture immediately sprung to mind. I sensed the Spirit of God say, "See!" Joy and delight filled my soul at this wonderful affirmation that I was where God wanted me to be. As I have walked the ministry journey, God's guidance and confirmation of each step has been affirmed through experiences such as this.

Recollections of tangible evidence serve to solidify the call. Such external affirmations from God attest to the deeper affirmation in your spirit. Through every test, reflect on the ways in which God moved to shape your call. His Holy Spirit will reinforce a certainty deep within you. No matter how intense the fight, how tumultuous the storm, you are kept in steadfast obedience to his will.

The nature of the call

The call of God is always to a specific task even though the exact details of that task may not be evident in the early stages. There are exceptions but generally the nature of the task is not unappealing. There are those that say the work they are doing for God is carried out reluctantly, e.g., "I don't want to do this but I am doing this out of obedience." What pious nonsense! Nothing could be further from the truth. It is incongruent with the fact that God has *"created us anew in Christ Jesus, so that we can do the good things he planned for us long ago"* (Ephesians 2:10). Our purpose on this planet is to do "*the good things.*" Further, God created our purpose "*long ago*" before he created our person and "*before he created our person anew in Christ Jesus.*" This means each person is especially "wired" with a unique personality, gifts and abilities to fit the purpose he has set for us. It is being made anew in Christ that fully opens our hearts to and gives access to, his supernatural empowerment for that purpose.

Since doing his will is also *"good, pleasing and perfect"* (Romans 12:2), it stands that the outworking of it will be the means by which we experience the *"life in all its fullness"* (John 10:10) promised by Jesus. Yes, carrying out the will of God from the human perspective is challenging, demanding and costly. Yes, his cause is daunting. It is larger than life and requires your life. But in the process you find life and you bring life to others. Nothing compares with the sense of destiny found in that.

I believe the following three indicators are intrinsic in the nature of any task corresponding to the call:

It will excite your spirit

It is true that many of the great leaders in the Bible were initially reticent or reluctant to respond to God's call. However, whether the call is embraced eagerly or with apprehension, the obedient leader soon discovers that the will of God is not a grievous thing.

The call inevitably corresponds with the desire of the heart, desire which God himself has deposited there. To that extent the compliant heart will be drawn to obedience by a divine "want to" within. His call will relate to a ministry task which will both excite and energize. It will mean that despite the challenges, you will for the most part serve the call with passion and enthusiasm. In the process of its outworking, you will also find meaning, purpose and fulfillment.

It will be bigger than you

Don't imagine that God will ask you to do what you can do. He will ask you to do what you cannot do, so that you will depend on him for the doing of it. In this respect the call of God is overwhelming. It is both common and human to wrestle with feelings of personal inadequacy in the light of it. You want to embrace it but at the same time you want to run from it. The work God calls us to do is always bigger than us.

However, God never calls us without the promise of the wherewithal to carry it out. The work of God will never be accomplished by human effort alone, but by continual surrender to the empowerment of the Holy Spirit. The prerequisite to an obedient response when the call of God comes is one of faith. Faith believes that *"The one who calls you is faithful and he will do it"* (1 Thessalonians 5:24). Strength will be required to accomplish that which God sets before you – not your own strength, but the empowering grace of God who has called you.

It will be about the blessing of others

You are here to make a difference! We are to carry Christ's presence in such a way that individual lives and society are beneficially transformed and Christ's church built. Through you, others are introduced and exposed to Kingdom life and love. Through you, others are to be influenced to come into alignment with Kingdom principles and Christ's purpose for their own lives. Whatever the nature of the call, it will have that primary objective. When God called Abraham he said, *"I will bless you.... and I will make you a blessing to others"* (Genesis 12:2). In a general sense, that's God's call to all who follow Christ. You are blessed to be a blessing!

Chapter Two
Security in Identity

I was wheeling a cart full of groceries through a car park when my attention was caught by the whoops and yells of a group of young skateboarders exuberantly demonstrating their skills. Just over my right shoulder came a voice, "I'll have to talk to those guys. I've already told them to stop playing around in here. I'll have to get rid of them." This was a voice of authority, one of importance, from one who was obviously in charge. The voice followed close on my shoulder until I reached the car, popped the trunk and began unloading the groceries from the cart. It was then that I looked up and saw the badge of office proudly pinned to a puffed chest. The voice of authority belonged to a Cart Recovery Technician!

Most of us, if we are honest, can relate to the innate sense of inflated ego or elevated self-image that comes with the bearing of title, position, wealth or power. Such accomplishments in themselves are valid and honorable pursuits for progress and influence in life. However, they can also be trappings that feed our sense of self-worth and enhance our feelings of significance. They can serve to define who we are, not just in our own minds but also we hope, in the minds of others. Too often and probably more than we are prepared to admit, our quest for these things arises from a deep internal deficit in the human heart: the need for a sense of security in our identity. Identity answers the important question: "Who am I?" The search for the answer to that age old question is commonly wrapped up in what we do, rather than who we are. I suspect the cart recovery technician gained a fair bit of self-prestige from wearing that shiny badge.

Perhaps all of us carry a sense of insecurity in our identity, at least to a degree. It is just a matter of where we might stand on the continuum. Undoubtedly the less secure we are in our identity, the more driven we will be in our quest for that identity to be affirmed. We will strive vigorously in the pursuit of external trappings in the attempt to define who we are.

Lost from the beginning

Identity is defined as the fact of being the same in all respects, who a person is, or what a thing is, which are true under all circumstances. It may surprise you to know that the concept of identity has been with us from the time of creation. When God made his decision to create humankind, he said, *"Let us make people in our image to be like ourselves"* (Genesis 1:26). In the beginning the crucial issue of Adam and Eve's identity was found in their likeness and relationship to God. Their core identity was held secure by that image. It was exactly that image or sense of identity that became the focal point of Satan's attack saying to Eve, *"You will become like God when you eat it* [the fruit of the tree of knowledge of good and evil]. *You will become just like God."* (Genesis 3:5).

In the environment of free will in which they were created, Adam and Eve surrendered to the doubt raised by Satan's probe at the core of their being. They were in fact already like God. There was nothing further to be achieved in terms of their true being, but the first human couple from whom we are all derived succumbed to the insidious and invasive nature of doubt. As a consequence, the image of God in which they were created was broken and their identity found in relationship with him was severed.

The consequences were life changing. On hearing the Lord God walking in the Garden of Eden, they now tried to hide from him among the trees. No longer sure of their standing before him, they were confused, afraid, and uncertain in their identity. Then came the searching question (pun intended): *"The Lord God called to Adam 'Where are you?'"* (Genesis 3:8). This was not a seeking after his whereabouts but more of a question in regard to the state of the heart. *"Where are you?"* was the same as, "Who are you?" God of course knew the answer, but the question poignantly reinforced for Adam the shift that had taken place in his very nature, the loss of connection to his true identity.

Ever since that dramatic moment, humankind has sought to recapture what has been lost. The void lies deep within our human psyche, passed down through the generations. The search for identity has become the primary driver for human significance, value and meaning in each person's life. The answer for many is not easily found while the search is opposed, confused and clouded on every front.

The identity issue is still the target of Satan's attack against humanity. He capitalizes on the void left by our broken image. Ironically, he himself promises to fulfill it. In our search for identity he deceptively leads us down a myriad of deceptive pathways that promise to fulfill the need but which always inevitably and ultimately disappoint.

The search for identity

We may not be fully aware of it but the gnawing quest for identity permeates every area of our life. On a personal level our looks, our clothes, the place we live, the car we drive, our work, our ministry, our families and relationships all tend to shape who we are.

When it comes to nations, whether it is a war or a football game, the contest is not just about conquest. It is also about reinforcing identity. For example, the ongoing conflict in the Middle East between Palestine and Israel is not a simple argument about geographical boundaries. It concerns the cultural identity of each side as a nation and the desire to be affirmed and defined by possessing their own land or territory.

Why is it that my rugby-mad nation of New Zealand plummets into a kind of depression when its national team, the All Blacks, loses a World Cup match? It is just a game after all. So it is, but when we lose, we feel our national identity has taken a hit and it hurts. Walk down the streets of Fiji (another fanatical rugby nation) and someone is bound to ask, "Where are you from?" Mention New Zealand and a typical response is, "Ah, All Blacks aye!" The association is made. The All Blacks for some New Zealanders represent and define who we are as a nation. The search for identity is intrinsic to every human endeavor.

Even the debate surrounding the Lord Jesus Christ revolved (and still does) around the single issue of identity – his! This debate drew the attention of kings and shepherds at his birth. During his ministry it drew the wonder of the common people and the wrath of the Pharisees. It resulted in a Roman cross at his death. The intense intrigue surrounding Christ's person was understood by Jesus himself who asked his disciples *"Who do people say that the Son of man is? 'Well,' they replied, 'some say John the Baptist, some say Elijah, and others say Jeremiah or one of the other prophets.' Then he asked them, "Who do you say I am?" Simon Peter answered, "You are the Messiah, the Son of the Living God"* (Matthew 16:10-16).

This question was not asked by Jesus for his own sake but for theirs. Security in his own identity had already been proven. It had been tested by the Devil using the same strategy as he had used against Eve in the garden. It had been attested by the Father who declared at Jesus' baptism, *"This is my beloved Son."*

The identity issue concerning Christ relates to the identity issue of our own hearts. Knowing who Jesus is becomes the pathway to knowing who we are.

The challenge around identity

It was the refusal of the religious authorities of the day to accept Christ's real identity that led to his crucifixion. Satan must have seen Jesus' death as yet another great victory, a moment of triumph in his relentless campaign of destruction with its strategy of identity confusion. Yet the cross was God's master plan. It was the way of God's purpose and power to restore the broken image of the human heart and spirit. When we place our faith and trust in Christ, God's own Son and true image bearer of the Father, a new image or identity is received. A miraculous transaction takes place. Our old broken and flawed identity is exchanged for a brand new one in restored relationship with the Father. The apostle Paul sums it up nicely: *"What this means is that those who become Christians become new persons. They are not the same any more, for the old life has gone. A new life has begun"* (1 Corinthians 5:17). Note that Paul describes the miracle we call "salvation" both as an event and a process. In one action by the Holy Spirit we are a new person.

However, that new life has to be worked out by the ongoing action of the Holy Spirit. Paul says, *"And as the Spirit works within us, we become more and more like him and reflect his glory even more"* (1 Corinthians 3:18).

While our true positional identity has been restored, the full revelation, realization, and recovery of that identity is a journey that will occur only over time. I love those little children's tee shirts that say, "Be patient, God isn't finished with me yet." Those words sum up our spiritual walk, personally and in ministry. Our new identity has to be shaped, fashioned and molded like a sculpture or painting at the hands of the Master Artist.

We all have some growing to do. We all come into our positions of ministry leadership still "under construction." We all carry still buried or masked insecurities of our previous flawed and marred identity, yet to be exposed and healed.

Gaining an awareness of these insecurities and how they drive or confuse our view of who we are and what we do is paramount to ministry survival. Make no mistake; any insecurity around your identity will be your Achilles heel. The enemy will attack any area of vulnerability he can to cause you to come unstuck in ministry.

To avoid the traps, the first helpful step is to own up to the fact that you are likely to be carrying insecurity issues to some degree. The next is to candidly reflect and assess the extent to which these have become part of your internal motivation for ministry leadership. To be driven by identity issues will have major consequences for your ministry, because it will affect the way your leadership is carried out. Any self-evaluation should include an examination of the way you relate to people and how you react to leadership challenges when the pressure is on.

Some characteristics of insecurity in identity

Some insight into the characteristics of insecurity within your sense of identity will prove helpful in carrying out a self-analysis. The indicators of insecurity relating to your identity are not visible unless you are willing to be brutally honest with yourself and learn how to recognize them.

The following list is not exhaustive but is simply compiled from those I have identified in my own journey towards wholeness or those I have observed in others. At this point allow me to express a caution. Because the heart is deceptive above all else, we often cannot see our own flaws or blind spots. A trusted friend or mentor may help you to see and acknowledge if any of the following apply to you.

Placing an undue importance on position or title

Just like the cart technician, at one stage in my ministry my own sense of value or worth was very much derived from my title or my position as "Pastor" of the church. I remember receiving ministerial accreditation from the denomination I was in and the sense of inflated self-importance I felt. I was a "Reverend." I even filed away as a keepsake the letter addressed to me in that form.

The importance of title or position is often exaggerated in the minds of the insecure. I once had to almost wrestle a gold "Head Deacon" badge off a leader in a team I had inherited. Another pastoral team member continually upset staff by insisting that he be addressed as "Pastor" even around the office.

Titles of course delineate position, function and sometimes convey power and authority. When a leader has to flaunt his or her title, it is a sign of insecurity. The title becomes an external affirmation of the internal value being sought. The title is a self-image booster. The fact is, the more secure ministry leader with a healthier self-image will be unaffected by the use or non-use of titles.

A pastor once told me that he realized he had moved further along the security continuum when he realized he no longer had to be identified as the "Pastor of the Church" and was comfortable just "being in his own skin." Having reached that place, his identity was not found in clinging to title and position. God was then able to eventually lead him into an itinerant prophetic ministry with considerable international influence.

Being performance oriented

All of us want to feel that we are succeeding at what we do. When God calls us to ministry leadership, I don't believe for one moment that he doesn't want us to succeed. Jesus himself said, *"My disciples produce much fruit. This brings great glory to my Father"* (John 15:8). The challenge for us is this: what is the definition of "much fruit" in the context of our own ministry leadership and who is really getting the glory?

The leader who is insecure will often be confused in his perception of what success is and blind to the primary internal motivation that drives him: specifically, the need to affirm his own sense of worth by what he has accomplished. When results don't measure up to the leader's perceptions of success, this reflects directly on his self-image and identity. The feeling of being a failure gnaws at the spirit, propagating the lie, "you are not measuring up." The consequence is to work even harder and longer to get the desired results. You must prove your value to the world. This inevitably leads to the all too common experience of burnout in ministry.

Burnout often occurs after a prolonged period of physical and emotional effort, in an attempt to turn around what the leader perceives as unproductive or unsuccessful ministry. Personal health and too often family relationships are the precious sacrifices laid on the altar. The term "workaholic" applies just as well in the ministry context as it does in the secular.

When ministry becomes the leader's primary shaper of identity, it insidiously metamorphoses into something that consumes and depletes the personal world of the leader and those around him. People are seen as commodities to be utilized to enhance the leader's own performance and image. The goal of production (albeit subliminal in the mind of the leader) becomes the agenda. When priority is focused on the leader's needs and desires in terms of time, effort and energy, there is a real danger of others being dragged down with the leader. Everyone involved becomes tired, disheartened and discouraged in the quest to meet unrealistic goals and expectations, all for the sake of the insecure leader's ego.

Needing to be needed

A wise counsellor once gave me a profound warning: "Ministry is a bottomless pit and people will kill you if you let them." Ministry leadership by its nature is holistic in its intent. It includes an ongoing investment in the spiritual growth and the physical and emotional well-being of the people entrusted to the leader's care. This is a tall order. It is never meant to be carried by a leader alone. However, the leader struggling for identity and self-worth falls into some kind of martyr complex when it comes to the needs of the people. Value is gained by "needing to be needed." This reveals itself in the inability to say "no." The failure to draw appropriate boundaries will allow the demands of ministry to intrude into the leader's personal and family life.

I well recall in my early years of ministry how I allowed personal time, family times, even meal times to be interrupted by phone calls, unannounced visits and the pastoral expectations of the people. Then there were the meetings and yet more meetings about ministry matters that always seemed to have to be held "after hours." I was out most nights of the week.

While the love for people and the desire to see their needs realized is essential for healthy leadership, something is wrong when this availability knows no bounds. If you find yourself saying "yes" too easily and often when you know you should say "no," you are probably feeling insecurity in your identity and are in reality ministering for love instead of from love. You need to be needed to feed your lack of internal worth and value. You are Superman, ready to leap to the rescue when the call for help is sounded.

Failure to delegate and empower others

Insecure leadership tends to exercise a high degree of control and a "hands on" approach to ministry. The leader will often go through the motions of delegation to others but won't give empowerment along with it to fulfill the task. Nothing can be more frustrating or disheartening than to be given a responsibility and then have that same leader constantly inputting, interfering or changing things. In reality this is not delegating at all. You have passed on a responsibility, yes, but you have not passed on the authority and freedom needed to carry things out.

It is fair enough to delegate responsibility within clearly defined parameters but if you find yourself constantly "putting your oar in," you are a controlling leader with issues of insecurity. This same sense of insecurity will cause a leader to feel threatened by the success of others, and reluctant to publicly affirm or acknowledge the efforts of the team or other leaders.

This kind of control is born out of the need to make others believe that nothing of dynamic significance occurs within the church or in the lives of others apart from the insecure leader's own involvement.

Having a high need for visibility

We all understand our own personal challenges with pride. The human ego is a powerful thing. While there are positive aspects to pride, when it becomes the "friend" of insecurity, it will act the part of greatness to mask the feeling of smallness inside. Identity by its very nature craves affirmation. This drive sometimes uncomfortably sits within our motivations for ministry leadership which revolve around desires that are self-seeking and actions which are self-promoting.

The quest for prominence is not something we would readily own up to. You know it is there when you are miffed because you haven't been allocated VIP seating at the conference or invited up to the green room to hang with the "big boys" (assuming you aren't one of the big boys). Maybe you find yourself sulking because you didn't get the recognition or praise you were expecting. Worse still, you are feeling resentful at others receiving the attention and the bouquets. I remember the great Pastor Peter Morrow saying, "Not all are called to prominence but everyone is called to significance" – yet so many feel they must have the former to experience the latter. You see it on Facebook, blogs and Twitter, where great effort is put into the promotion of "my ministry successes," name-dropping, sycophantic ramblings and the regurgitation of one's own praise.

When tempted to elevate our ministry successes, we are to be reminded of the Apostle Paul's advice: "*The person who wishes to boast should boast only of what the Lord has done*" (2 Corinthians 10:13), and Jesus' sober reminder that, *"For apart from me you can do nothing"* (John 15:5).

The desire for personal visibility propagates a territorial approach which emphasizes "my ministry." This leads to the building of "my kingdom," which is aggressively protected when that kingdom is threatened. The "my ministry" syndrome is a real challenge to integrity. I have gotten into the habit of asking God to examine my own heart and show me those moments when my motivation and attitudes have crossed the boundary. You don't want to get to the end of the journey only to discover that instead of building the House of God to make his name great, you have built a Tower of Babel in order to make your own name great!

To be transparent before God about the ego's tendency to desire visibility is a healthy self-awareness to have. To remind yourself that what God has called you to do is not to be regarded as "your ministry" or "your church" but as "his ministry" or "his church." This will keep you from self-seeking and help you stay on track. Just be aware that vanity itself can be a subtle but primary motivator in ministry.

Riding the emotional roller coaster

Ministry leadership has its ups and downs. There are times when things are going well. There are times when things are not going so well. Sometimes things are just going downright badly. That's the nature of ministry. Get used to it. It will never be any different than that.

It has been said that the ministry cycle of a church involves three seasons: the lift, sift, and shift. Give me the "lift" any day! The reality is seasons of sift and shift are inevitable. These seasons of tension, pain, pressure and perceived unproductivity occur as part of the normal growth cycle. Jesus reminds us that pruning has to happen if greater fruitfulness is to come (c.f. John 15).

Struggles with identity mean these oscillations in ministry will result in corresponding oscillations in our emotional life. During the lift we are emotionally up. During the times of sift and shift, we are stressed and depressed. Deep insecurity issues will cause you to ride that emotional roller coaster from week to week. If attendance is up, you are up; if it is down, you are down. If you feel you have preached well, all is well. If you haven't, then all is not well.

If you relate to this, it is a sign your inner life needs some transformation. You cannot continue to live like that. This kind of emotional yo-yoing wreaks havoc on your physical and psychological health, leading to exhaustion.

I am not advocating an emotionless response to the joys and demands of ministry but a certain amount of emotional equilibrium is required if your ministry is going to be sustained. However, if your sense of value and worth is reliant on the growth seasons of ministry productivity and you cave in during the times of pruning and unproductivity, you have to acknowledge that you have an identity problem.

Identity is found apart from call

As stated previously, true security in identity is found in who we are *in* Christ. It is not found in what we do *for* him. It is the ongoing pursuit of intimacy in that relationship that assures us with a sense of personal value, place and purpose. From the moment we surrender our lives to Christ and are born again by his Spirit into son-ship, we are first and foremost a child of God. As mentioned earlier, the realization of this truth is something of a process but it is God's desire that we fully grasp it as "*his Holy Spirit speaks to us deep in our hearts and tells us we are his children*" (Romans 8:16).

I vividly recall my own moment of knowing God as my Father. The experience of that revelation through Jesus Christ is indelibly printed on my heart. In truth I don't have words to adequately describe the encounter but it turned my life around forever.

There was no particular crisis occurring in my life (as is often required before many look to God). I was happily married with two beautiful sons and a satisfying career. At the invitation of a work colleague, who was a Christian, I found myself somewhat reluctantly attending the first ever Full Gospel Business Men's dinner held in Pakuranga, Auckland. We had been having the occasional God conversations that had arisen out of the inquiry of my own heart.

Even though life was going well, I still knew an emptiness inside. I often reflected on the big questions in life. "What's it [life] all about? Why are we here? What happens when we die?" Even brain freeze questions were up for debate: "What is beyond the universe? What was before the universe? If nothing, was that in fact something?"

I can't imagine anyone going through life without considering such concerns. It puzzles me that many just live within the microcosm of the personal universe of self without the desire to explore beyond their own world. This is not a judgement but merely an observation. Subsequent spiritual insight allows me to see that my own quest for truth was not initiated by my own volition but by God himself. Jesus said, *"For people can't come to me unless the Father who sent me draws them to me"* (John 6:44). My searching was only a response to the Spirit's wooing.

The meal was great, the singing with a group of men before the meal was weird (don't men just sing at parties or football matches?). However, the story of a transformed life by the power of the Gospel told by lawyer and soon to become one of New Zealand's most prominent evangelists, Bill Subritsky, resonated deeply within me. I remember suddenly being impacted by the revelation of the nature of my own sin and my need of rescue from that. There came a strong sense of knowing that the answers to those questions gnawing in my spirit were to be found in the receiving of Christ into my life.

The invitation to do that came. Everyone sat at his table, eyes closed. "Please stand if you would like to give your life to Jesus." My heart was pounding. My fingers gripped the edges of the table. An internal wrestling match was taking place, "This is what you need to do! No! This is crazy! Stay where you are!" The battle raged. I peeked to see if anyone had stood. There were some. Good! That would make it easier! The drawing was intense, compelling, not in the sense of feeling forced but in the sense of a growing "want to" inside. Heart pounding, feeling like it would explode in my chest, I released my grip from the table and stood. A moment passed; then Bill led us all in a simple prayer of commitment receiving Christ as Lord and Savior.

As I repeated the words, something almost indescribable happened. My fast beating heart slowed to a steady beat. Warmth like a blanket of love came down from above and enveloped my being. I was aware of the most incredible peace I have ever experienced (this remained with me for weeks afterwards). When I opened my eyes, the whole room seemed filled with light. I could hardly see except to make out the blurred vision of the smiling face of the friend who had brought me. He was vigorously shaking my hand. In that moment I understood one thing. God was absolutely real and he was with me.

When God gives us his Spirit, we are *"adopted into his family, calling him Father, dear Father"* (Romans 8:15). The sense of security as a son of the Father is unsurpassable as an anchor for this life. However, despite my own overwhelming experience of the Father's love in my first encounter with him, the journey to a fuller understanding and experience of that truth has been a continuing work of the Holy Spirit.

It may largely depend on the degree of insecurity in identity that you bring with you when you are adopted into God's family. My own parents split up when I was about six years old. Contact with my father was not re-established until about thirty years afterwards. A father's hug is foreign to me as are the words, "Son, I love you."

Our perceptions of God can be distorted by the experiences of our less than perfect human fathers. Even after many years of walking with Christ I confess that a residual vulnerability still remains. Each time it is exposed it is countered and further healed by the truth of God's word and by tangible experiences of his love. The apostle Paul prayed, *"May you experience the love of Christ"* (Ephesians 3:19). To experience God's love is to know him by firsthand acquaintance and subjective experience. There is nothing like the truth of God's word validated by the touch of God's presence to bring reassurance.

God loves you and has put a value on you that no role or office or any worldly success can exceed. He has paid a price of inestimable value in the sacrifice of his Son, Jesus Christ, to purchase you. Jesus said, *"You didn't choose me, I chose you"* (John 15:16). Paul reiterates this truth saying, *"For God knew his people in advance, and he chose them"* (Romans 8:29). The Greek word for "chose" is *eklogomai,* which means *to select as the recipient of special favors and privilege.*

You have been specially selected. It is the kind of special selection taken with the great love and care that a guy might take in choosing an engagement ring for the girl he wishes to marry. The serious contemplation of that thought overwhelmingly affirms identity. Think of it! Out of all the billions of people who have ever lived or who are still yet to live since the beginning of creation, God looked down through time and said, "I choose you!"

Before we are saved, we perform to get an identity so we are accepted. After we are saved, we begin to find out we are accepted and out of that reality comes our performance.[1] When we fully understand our identity in Christ, we are free to invest ourselves in that which he has called us to do. God has vested us with the honor and privilege of having him as our Creator, Father, Redeemer and Comforter. Our value is found in him. The more we grasp this, the less we try to have to prove ourselves to others. Our security rests entirely in who we are in Christ, not in what we do or achieve. This connection with God is the inner quest of our soul. We want to have what we had in the beginning. True identity and therefore true security are only found in an ongoing and deepening relationship with Christ.

End note:

[1]. Bill Johnson, *Hosting the Presence, Unveiling Heaven's Agenda.* Destiny Image Publishers, Shippensburg, USA, 2012, page 189.

Chapter Three
Being a Leader Who Can Follow

It is important for me to note that much of this chapter has been strongly influenced not just from my own observations and experiences but by one of the best books I have ever read on the subject, *"Follow the Leader"* by Simon McIntyre.[1] This is a must read for any aspiring leader who wants to understand the dynamics of being a leader who can follow.

Not everyone called to ministry leadership will find themselves in a primary leadership role. Even when this is the ultimate destiny for you, the pathway will most likely mean serving first as part of a team, serving the vision of another. In that context you will need to demonstrate the attitude and art of being a follower. The ability to grasp this principle is one of the key factors in leadership promotion. The inability to grasp it will be an impediment to your progress or even the collapse of your ministry journey altogether. It was Ed Cole who said: "We need to learn to be faithful to that which is another man's." This exemplifies the principle that it is those who prove to be good and faithful servants who are rewarded with greater authority, work and responsibility. If we can submit ourselves to administer and interpret the vision of another, we set ourselves up for the fulfillment of our own dreams and visions in the future.

Being able to care for someone else's vision and property sounds straightforward enough, but it does challenge the desire for our own advancement and orientation towards self-promotion. We are often sold the idea that unless we become the prime leader we have fallen short of fulfilling our potential.

The amazingly fruitful and varied life of Joseph, who was called to leadership is a powerful challenge to this mindset.

Joseph began his journey to leadership as a slave caring for the property of another. Joseph from an early age had carried the God-given aspiration for leadership in his heart. Even so, he didn't strive for it, engineer circumstances or manipulate others for it. He simply served faithfully and with integrity in the midst of a series of adverse and challenging circumstances unjustifiably thrust upon him. As a consequence, *"The Lord was with Joseph and blessed him greatly as he served in the home of his Egyptian master"* (Genesis 39:2). Ultimately Joseph ended up in a position of extremely high prominence and authority over the nation itself:

"I [Pharaoh] *hereby appoint you to direct this project. You will manage my household and organize all my people. Only I will have a rank higher than yours"* (Genesis 41:40).

Joseph's story shows that even if you are called to be a "top dog" eventually, the pathway is that of humble, loyal and faithful service to another.

As a senior leader in ministry I place a high value on loyalty within the leadership team. Loyalty exists when everyone on the team understands the significance of being able to follow. This expectation is not based on my insecurities (yes, I do have them and like you are working on them), but out of the realization that loyalty, not just to my leadership but to the common vision and the team itself, is essential. Without it, things are just not going to work.

By loyalty I don't mean that I surround myself with "yes men" or demand blind allegiance. In fact, loyalty can only be tested in the context of disagreement or if there is an opportunity to be disloyal.

Loyalty as a follower is the ability to hold together in unity, during the good times and the tough times. It is the willingness to lay down personal agendas and to find agreement out of disagreement. It is never allowing a contrary opinion to succumb to that of a contrary spirit. It is the attitude that will allow you to speak and act only for the common good of the leader, the vision and team you serve.

Jesus told his disciples, *"You have remained true to me in my time of trial. And just as my Father has granted me a Kingdom, I now grant you the right to eat and drink at my table in that Kingdom. And you will sit on the twelve thrones, judging the tribes of Israel"* (Luke 22:29). The promise is eschatological but the principle is clear. The disciples had stuck with him through thick and thin when others had deserted him and spoken against him. Even when they didn't quite understand what was going on, they remained loyal. The reward for that kind of followership is leadership authority. Loyalty to those over you is an absolutely crucial quality for ongoing personal advancement. If you understand what it is to come under authority, God can trust you to be given authority.

Traps to be avoided

Given the human propensity for self-promotion, there are a number of pitfalls those aspiring to ministry leadership need to be aware of. To fall into any of the following traps will mean the self-sabotage of your ministry leadership destiny.

Betrayal of trust

All of us in leadership need to appreciate that along with leadership authority, the power and responsibility associated with the role has been entrusted to us. In the first instance the gift of leadership has been bestowed upon us by God, but the recognition and ordination of that leadership gift in most cases has been delegated to us by those in the church already in authority over us. Leadership is not something that should bring with it an expectation of personal entitlement. It should instead inspire a sense of personal responsibility that ensures the good stewardship of the gift entrusted to you.

It has always amazed me how quickly that is forgotten by some. Again and again I have seen aspiring leaders get carried away with their own sense of importance and entitlement. Self-serving motives (arising from insecurity in identity) drive them to seek greater influence by undermining and criticizing the very authority that appointed them in the first place. Over time they may establish their own vision outside of the vision they were first empowered to serve. In short, they believe they can do better. That in fact might be true, but "biting the hand that feeds you" is not going to further your influence or advancement.

I once appointed a pastor to my team whom I gave the authority to preach. He preached one Sunday when I was away and on my return I asked him how it went. His reply astounded me, "They liked *my* vision." To proclaim an alternative vision to the one you are called to serve is to create division. That was my first inkling he was not really following. Over time, a critical and rebellious spirit surfaced. This ultimately led to his downfall and the departure of some who liked "his vision." The sad thing is that he was genuinely called and gifted. My heart was to help him realize that call but he stumbled by betraying the trust given to him. To this day, his aspirations for greater ministry leadership responsibility have never been realized. I often wonder what might have been if he had been faithful to that trust and to the principle of being able to follow.

Every leader must understand that they are in some sense a follower and therefore accountable for that following. Authority is passed down by God's appointed authority in his church. It is prudent to appreciate then that those ordained to empower, are also ordained to disempower.

Abuse of influence

Positions of ministry leadership can sometimes involve high profile roles that come with considerable influence. Most leaders by nature are gatherers. It is natural for people to be attracted to a particular leadership style or personality, and when individual leaders use their power to attract and collectively draw people together in a common vision, the church can see incredible growth.

This power to gather can be misappropriated by using it to gain your own following at the expense of the leader over you. Sadly, too many leaders have abused that power to divide the church even to the point of leaving and taking their followers with them. Nothing is more heart wrenching to the church than to experience the devastation associated with that kind of split. Interestingly, in the great majority of cases I have observed in my years of ministry, the recalcitrant leader's alternative and usually independent ministry has seen little or no growth. Often the work has ultimately faltered.

Absalom's rebellion against his father King David is a prime example of abuse of influence by a leader invested with considerable power and authority simply as the king's son. He appears to have had everything going for him including good looks and a winning personality. However, Absalom, like most who abuse trust, had his own agenda. He wanted to be king and used his position and gifts to serve his own ends. Over a period of four years he worked furtively to seed the idea in the minds of the people that he would be a more accessible, attentive, sympathetic and caring king than his father. He sided with people's complaints and pointed out supposed deficiencies in the king's ability to lead. He curried favor with the people, putting aside the formalities of office to embrace them as an understanding and endearing friend. *"In this way, Absalom stole the hearts of all the people of Israel"* (2 Samuel 15:6).

Absalom almost succeeded in his attempt. Such was Absalom's influence that a messenger informed King David: *"All Israel has joined Absalom in a conspiracy against you"* (2 Samuel 15:13). Fortunately, the king's bodyguard along with his Gittite friend and ally, Ittai, captain of six hundred fighting men, still stood with David. More importantly, he had with him the presence of God symbolized by the carrying of the Ark of the Covenant. Even so, in an amazing expression of trust in God for his ultimate destiny, David ordered the Ark of God to be returned to Jerusalem, saying: *"If the Lord sees fit ...he will bring me back to see the Ark and the Tabernacle again. But if he is through with me, then let him do what seems best to him"* (2 Samuel 16:25-26).

David's response is a profound example to any leader facing a challenge to his leadership. He did not resign himself to the relinquishment of his kingship without a fight, but neither did he desperately cling to it. Ultimately, he completely trusted God with it. When a leader knows God has called and appointed him, he knows that God will also hold secure that appointment.

God had not finished with David and the outcome of the saga was the quashing of the rebellion and Absalom's death. The latter David deeply laments. Overcome with intense grief and emotion he burst into tears; *"O my son Absalom! My son, my son Absalom! If only I could have died instead of you!"* (2 Samuel 19: 33).

Most senior leaders who have been in ministry for any length of time have felt the grief of the loss of a "son" whom they have given themselves to and entrusted with power and authority, only to have that trust betrayed. It is not just the betrayal and the loss of a son that hurts. It is the loss of that son's ministry inheritance, the "what might have been" that brings sadness.

In the end, every aspiring leader should realize that to allow personal ambition to usurp the authority over him in order to advance in the process betrays that trust given to him. Such disregard brings the risk of dire consequences for the leader's own future ministry progress.

Impatience for promotion

Betrayal often arises when there is an impatience for promotion. We may tend to want advancement in leadership far sooner than we are ready for it. Impatience fueled by the ambition for self-promotion can be a pathway to ministry disaster.

Korah, who rebelled against the divinely appointed leadership of Moses, typifies the methods followed by those who pursue their own ends. Korah's strategy for self-promotion drove him to rise up against the existing leadership: *"They incited a rebellion against Moses involving 250 other prominent leaders, all members of the assembly"* (Numbers 16:2). The self-promoting leader will be the consummate networker, building relationships with others they deem to be influential and helpful to their cause. Once confident of support, the recalcitrant leader will begin to question and criticize the existing leadership among his "influential friends." He will then present that complaint to the leader justifying the action with the weighty but deceptive argument that, "A lot of people feel this way." Korah and his group "went to Moses and Aaron and said, *"You have gone too far! Everyone in Israel has been set apart by the Lord, and he is with all of us"* (Numbers 16:3a).

It was the *"you have gone too far"* lie that sought to directly undermine Moses' leadership. Korah was essentially saying that he had as much right to exercise leadership as Moses himself *and* accused Moses of getting carried away with his authority: *"What right do you have to act as though you are greater than anyone else, among all these people of the Lord?* (Numbers 16:3b).

Every lie has a kernel of truth to give it credibility. We may well "all be set apart" by the Lord, but we are not all set apart for the same function or role among God's people. Korah was stretching the truth under the guise of egalitarian concerns to push his own ambition. He was not satisfied with the already significant position he had been given. He wanted greater authority and prominence, he wanted the platform, he wanted to "preach more." As the saga unwinds to its conclusion, Korah and his rebellious cohorts find themselves in a bit of a hole and go down forever in history as a salutary lesson for those whose personal ambitions and actions are outside of God's timing or purpose.

God may well have for you greater leadership responsibility to come, but it is always best to be patient and wait for the Lord to promote. Don't ever resort to manipulation and coercion to fulfill your ambition. Follow David's exhortation: *"Don't be impatient for the Lord to act! Travel steadily along his path. He will honor you, giving you the land* " (Psalm 37:34).

Receiving complaints about your leader

When someone wants to complain to you about your leader, you are put into the position where your response can either expose or protect him. The idea is always to maintain your own integrity as a follower. If the complaint is unjustified, it is easy if you are loyal to back your leader and help the complainant see things from the leader's perspective. You may help to bring clarity and understanding around the issue of concern.

The challenge really comes if you see there is some validity to the complaint. The danger is in the giving of alignment to the view point, e.g. "I know what you mean," thereby reinforcing the leader's weakness and justification of the complaint. This causes the one with the complaint to transfer his or her allegiance to you. This is how Absalom began his pathway of rebellion against David. Absalom would say to those bringing their grievances to him, *"You have a strong case here!"* You just don't want to go there.

So what do you do? It is best not to express an opinion of sympathetic support at all. However, as with an invalid complaint, allow the person to feel that they have been heard and understood. Next, try to help them see matters from the leader's perspective, especially in regard to the positive intent behind a leader's words or actions. In other words, seek to remain faithful to your leader and endeavor to smooth over the leader's shortcomings. Protect your leader as far as possible by watching his back and dealing with the matter on his behalf. (Please note that I am not talking about covering up illegal, unethical or immoral behavior).

There may be times when you have to protect the leader from himself. If you honestly feel that the complaint has sufficient substance to warrant the leader's attention, then it is better to come to him with a positive solution to the issue. Don't just dump another criticism or problem on him. There are constructive ways of saying things. Perhaps the way of approach is in the way Jethro sidled up to Moses to give him advice about his leadership style and methodology:

"This is not good!" his father in law exclaimed. "You are going to wear yourself out and the people too. This job is too heavy a burden for you to handle by yourself. Now let me give you a word of advice..." (Exodus 18:17-18).

Jethro gave Moses a lesson on the importance of delegation, approaching him respectfully and with caring concern. He tackled the issue by emphasizing the advantages of the needed adjustment to Moses himself as well as the advantages to the people.

Most leaders will receive guidance from those whom they know to be faithful and who are acting in their best interests. Secure leaders will give this kind of access. "Security allows the ability to listen to and take on board another's point of view."[2] It is only insecurity that will react defensively with the response, "I know better!"[3]

As followers, we should not be afraid to confront leadership decisions or actions when necessary, around real issues of concern. To do this takes courage and candor but if you can't do this, you will not follow by willing submission but by cowering coercion. You will follow from a place of frustration and resentment under an umbrella of misery.

If the leader remains fixed in his view, it may just be a matter of sucking it up and getting on with it. The last thing you want to do is self-sabotage your own life and ministry because you have decided to highlight the deficiencies of your leader and undermine his authority. Work hard at maintaining your integrity, pray for your leader and allow God to work it out.

Being too familiar

Leaders should be honored and respected. The concept of honoring leaders is foreign in my New Zealand culture compared to many others. Our classless and egalitarian ideals mean the idea of honoring leaders may not be popular with many. I know of leaders so affected by this view they won't allow themselves to be addressed as "Pastor" because they don't want to be seen as set apart from the rest of the congregation. While I would never insist on it for myself, I make a point of honoring those carrying the pastoral office by addressing them in public settings as "Pastor" when it is appropriate to do so. For example, the regional director of the C3 Church in New Zealand is both my friend and my leader. In a social or more personal setting I address him by his first name. In a public gathering or more formal setting he is "Pastor." By doing this I am simply honoring the leadership office and function in this particular way. Giving honor to leadership is a principle advocated in Scripture. Leaders, especially those who preach and teach, are worthy of *"double honor"* (1 Timothy 5:17).

When we honor leadership we acknowledge it and celebrate it. It is stated as a value in the church. This issue of giving honor can be a struggle at the leadership team level. Good teams tend to develop a reasonably deep level of friendship. This is a healthy thing but it can work detrimentally if the balance between friendship and respect is not maintained. Be aware that friendship with those over you has the power to erode authority and respect, if allowed to.

I once had to make a downward adjustment to a leader's ministry responsibility as a matter of discipline. The response to this was, "I thought we were friends!" The presumption was that friendship meant license, i.e., the rules can be relaxed because of the friendship. It is important to work out the boundaries in your situation. Over-familiarity towards your leader in the wrong context can thwart your ministry leadership progress because it won't allow easy submission to direction and discipleship.

All of the above indicators of the inability to follow are interrelated. The list is by no means exhaustive. They are, however, some of the more common traps for the unwary to fall into. In the final analysis, being a leader who is able to follow is an essential quality if you are ever to reach your fullest leadership potential.

End notes:

[1]Simon McIntyre, *Follow the Leader*. Inspire Publishing, Max Ministries Pty Ltd, Sydney, Australia, 2005 .

[2]Paul de Jong, *Isolating Insecurity*. Pindar, NZ, 2000, page 72.

[3]Paul de Jong, op.cit., page 73.

Chapter Four
Handling Criticism

Being in leadership requires visibility. When you put your head and shoulders up above the crowd it is inevitable that someone is going to want to take a pot shot at you. Criticism is endemic in our society. What is known as the "tall poppy syndrome" is real and pronounced in our culture. It is taken for granted that we knock our politicians, our bosses, our sports coaches and yes, in the church, our pastors and leaders. Unfortunately, as much as we might prefer it to be different, that is the reality. "Roast pastor" is a palatable delicacy for the discontented. We shouldn't be surprised, since the Biblical record is full of examples of God's appointed leaders coming under fire. Moses, David, Paul and others, even Jesus himself, had to withstand the barbs of criticism, so why not you?

Dr John Gilmore in his book, *Pastoral Politics,* lists twenty-one criticisms against Jesus:[1]

He was ignorant, uncultured, awkward (John 7:15)

He was not sent from God (John 9:16)

He was a revolutionary and radical (Luke 23: 2,5,14)

He was boastful and demeaning of others (Matthew 26:61)

He was a violator of the Law (John 9:24)

He was a bad example (Luke 6:2)

He taught self indulgence, gorged himself at meals, and drank heavily (Matthew 11:19)

He was of illegitimate birth (John 8:41, 48)

He was a liar (Matthew 26:59-6; 23:2; John 2:19-21)

His preaching brought "no blessing" (John 6:60-66)

He was difficult to follow and spoke over people's heads (John 2:19-21; 8:43-44)

He was a blasphemer (Matthew 26:65)

He was a criminal (John 18:30)

He was backward (John 7:4-5)

He was insane (Mark3:21; John 7:20; 8:48, 52)

He was in league with Satan and demons (John 8:48,52; Mark 3:22)

He was Satan's chief agent (Matt 12:24)

He was divisive (John 7:43; 9:16)

He preached strange doctrines (Luke 4:29)

Jesus put up with an incredible amount of flak. He also gave this sobering reminder: *"A servant is not greater than his master. Since they persecuted me, naturally they will persecute you"* (John 15:20).

Being in leadership takes great courage, the kind of courage that allows you to be set apart from the crowd in the point position that all leaders must assume. Realizing that criticism is par for the course is part of the armor necessary to deflect it. Criticism is the inevitable flak that goes with the job. If you can't get used to that reality, you can look forward to a life of misery. The secret is learning to toughen your heart without hardening your heart. For most of us that is easier said than done. Much of your ability to handle criticism will also depend on the strength of your call and the degree of security in your identity. Notwithstanding these two important areas for survival, there are ways of dealing with criticism so that it does not undermine your ministry journey or effectiveness.

Steps for handling criticism

Know the fight is not with the people

Because it is people who fire criticism at you, it is easy to see those people as the real enemy. The apostle Paul reminds us that whatever we face in the natural world as opposition to our ministry always has its spiritual origins. *"For we are not fighting against people made of flesh and blood"*, says Paul, *"but against the evil rulers and authorities of the unseen world, against those mighty powers of darkness who rule this world, and against wicked spirits in the heavenly realms"* (Ephesians 6:12).

Pastor Phil Pringle, Founder and President of C3 Global Movement and Senior Pastor of C3 Oxford Falls, Sydney, Australia, tells of his discovery of going to prayer and binding the Devil's influence over those who sought to criticize and undermine the church. Prayer for Pastor Phil has proven *"to be an amazingly powerful tool over the years."* [2] He has seen negative and critical attitudes changed almost immediately when the battle is fought on the spiritual plane. Pastor Phil regards this revelation as a *"secret to pastoring.*"[2] If you feel like shooting the people first and asking the questions later, transfer that aggression towards the Devil. He is the one behind it in the end. Praying first and giving God the opportunity to sort it out often rescues us from a lot of unnecessarily expended emotional energy trying to deal with criticism (and those hurling it) using only our own strength.

Don't let it distract you

It is strange how criticism has the power to take over your thoughts and actions if you allow it. Criticism can cut to the core of our being and wound us deeply. The innate insecurity of human nature means that if we receive nine e-mails of commendation and one e-mail of criticism, it will be that *one* which will dominate our thinking and keep us awake at night.

Criticism has the power to distort your perspective so that you totally lose focus. Most critics will of course argue that "a lot of people feel this way." Take that on board and you may begin to believe the whole church is up in arms. The irony is that it is the critic who has lost perspective. "A lot of people" can mean the two or three people in their own little world.

Be aware too that the voice of the critic is usually the most vociferous. Because it speaks loudly, we can be tempted to succumb to it with our time, effort and emotional energy. The old saying, "the squeaky wheel gets all the oil" is true. Criticism can consume us in a way that invariably distracts us from the greater task of leadership. All our energy goes into attempting to silence the voice and put out the fire. If that happens, the enemy has achieved his goal of keeping us from what matters.

Don't react defensively or offensively

I don't know about you, but when someone criticizes me, my natural inclination is to leap to my own defense. In my worst moments I want to attack back. In my experience, to spring immediately to your own defense merely looks like an attempt to duck for cover and protect your own butt. To go on the offensive by attacking the critic looks even worse and only escalates the matter. Either way, you are not helping things. Bottom line, don't allow yourself to overreact.

Most of the time criticism should be allowed to roll off like water off a duck's back. Most criticism tends to lose its force in time and eventually peter out. If the criticism has no basis, we can know that God will in his own way justify us and hold us secure. The truth, sooner or later, has the amazing propensity to come out.

Pastor Phil Pringle, quoting Charles Spurgeon's views on criticism, says there is one exception to this rule. That is when public criticism is made. In that case the criticism should be publicly responded to.[3] I know of a pastor in a small town who was criticized by an e-mail sent to other local pastors by the coordinator of the local minister's fraternal order. The criticism from his perspective was unjustified but his decision not to respond to it merely appeared as acquiescence and allowed the mud to stick. His standing in the local church community was detrimentally affected. The last thing any of us want is a fight in the public arena. On those rare occasions when it might be required, especially for the good of the church (not just for your reputation), ask the Lord to give you the power to respond with wisdom, integrity and strength.

Understand that critics speak out of their own pain

I firmly believe many who pick up the cudgel of criticism speak out of their own lack of self-worth, hurt and pain. I am no psychologist but I have this theory that those who seek to tear down others with their words are actually subconsciously building themselves up in the process. Think about it. The moment we speak negatively about another person, we are saying to ourselves and others that "I am not like that" or "I wouldn't do it that way." "I am better than that" or "I can do better than that." Understanding this lessens criticism's sting. The problem might well lie within them, not you.

Realize some criticism can be good for you

Criticism is very often an arrow that is intended to wound. Conversely, some criticism is for our benefit. We do well to listen and make the adjustments that will make us better in person and better at what we do. The question is how you tell the difference between what should be heeded and what should be discarded. The answer is surprisingly straightforward. It depends on who the critic is and how the criticism is made.

First, if the one who brings the criticism is someone you know to be a person of spiritual maturity and credibility and has your best interests at heart, it pays to listen. Usually there will be a historical relationship with that person where integrity, faithfulness and loyalty have been proven over time. They know your heart and they have stood with you because of who you are and often in spite of who you are.

Second, the criticism will be brought to you in love and with respect. Anyone who has to say to you, "I am bringing this in love," probably isn't. The obvious shouldn't need to be stated. The words and tone used will speak for themselves. It may come firmly and directly but more as a persuasive appeal than laying a charge at your feet. It will seek to build up as opposed to tearing down. Such advice is to be weighed and considered, and changes are to be made where necessary.

Leaders, as much as those they lead, are still disciples and need to be humble enough to receive correction. A humble leader will not act as if he is self-sufficient (or has it all together). He will not pretend to know all the answers and will put himself in a position to draw insights from others.[4]

Leaders need to be open, teachable and willing to be helped. We don't easily see where we might need to change and this is why God gives us each other. Others can help us see what we cannot. *Every* leader needs a mentor or trusted advisor to help them grow on the leadership journey. I have always been appreciative of those who love me enough to tell me what I need to hear, not just what I want to hear.

When and how to act against criticism

In my experience, much unjustified criticism against leadership relates to the leader's style and/or personality. It is often based on assumptions, presumptions and misunderstandings which have led to a sense of displacement or hurt in others, because they just don't know the leader's heart. Alternatively, critics may be at variance with the church's vision, ministry style and direction. Criticism may stem from a combination of these things.

With some forms of criticism, it is usually best just to live with the fact that not everyone will like you or understand you! If it is a small matter, learn to get over it and get on with it. If you are bothered by it, sometimes a heart to heart, one on one chat with the critic can clear the air and bring settlement. It is always a good thing to resolve differences in relationship when and where it is possible and profitable.

In all cases your intervention will depend on the nature of the criticism, taking into account who is behind it (i.e. what influence do they have) and whether or not it potentially threatens the unity, health and forward momentum of the church (as opposed to your own ego). The leader as shepherd of the flock has a primary responsibility to protect the church from the wolf. He needs to be able to take protective action in such cases.

Confronting people is never easy. Most of us would prefer not to go there. However, delaying or avoiding confrontation doesn't solve anything. It is prudent to take action sooner rather than later. If you are required to act, the following steps may prove helpful.

1. Get your facts right before you talk to the person who is the source of the criticism. If you only have half the story, you will flounder when they justify their position.

2. Be aware of your own shortcomings and any way in which you may have contributed to the issue. Be prepared to put those things right. Being prepared to say "I'm sorry" when you should goes a long way towards settlement.

3. Consult with your senior team and get their perspective on the matter. Always act from a place of agreement in terms of the nature and seriousness of the criticism and the steps needed to address it.

4. Sometimes appointing another trusted leader who may through relationship have influence over the critic can be a good move. Often they are able to present our case more objectively and forcibly than we can. This approach once worked for me

extremely effectively. As the new senior pastor of a church, I had only been in the position a very short time. I was still coming to grips with "who was who, in the zoo." A small group in the church decided they didn't like the way the new guy did things. One planned to call a meeting to incite the church to reconsider my appointment. I had not yet had enough time to build any sense of relationship or influence with the person leading the complaint. A key leader on my team who had an already established credibility with that person opted to intervene on my behalf. Without any involvement by me, the whole thing just petered out. If it has to be you, though, give careful thought to the place, the time, and what you want to say.

5. In general terms the guidelines in scripture (c.f. Matthew 18:15-17) should be followed. A one on one conversation with the critic should be the first approach. If things remain unresolved, it is wise to address the matter with another leader or two present. This is helpful from the point of view of corroborating what is said and done if necessary. If all this fails to bring resolution and the critic stays around to make trouble, Jesus' instruction is to take the matter to the church for judgement. By the church I mean the senior leadership in whom Jesus has invested the authority to govern. If you are the senior leader, make a call in conjunction with those who share oversight with you. You will want their wisdom and support on the matter. I have found that when the leadership team stands strong together, the church holds secure against any threat to its unity and well-being.

6. Again, and most important of all, is to pray for and hope for a healthy settlement for everyone concerned. In most cases, people just like to feel they have been heard and understood.

7. Always maintain an attitude of good will. Keep a "cool head and a warm heart" (not the other way around). Hold to the ideal but accept the reality that the sinfulness of human nature may scuttle the desired outcome, generally resulting in the critic leaving the church. In this case, do what you can to help them leave well, although sadly, the barb of their offense may make even that difficult for you. That said, I have no qualms about suggesting to people who are consistently unhappy with the church that they find another church where they can be happy.

End notes:

[1] Dr John Gilmore, *Pastoral Politics, Why Ministers Resign.* AMG Publishers, USA, 2002, pages 176-177.

[2] Phil Pringle, *You the Leader*, Pax Trading Ministries Pty Ltd, Dee Why NSW 2099, 1998, page 113.

[3] Phil Pringle, op. cit., page 113.

[4] John Haggai, *Lead On, Leadership that Endures in a Changing World.* Word Incorporated, Waco, Texas, 1986, page 63.

Chapter Five
The Emotional Challenge

Ministry leadership can only be sustained if there is the capacity to cope with the high emotional demands of ministry responsibility. The role brings with it incredible highs and devastating lows. While the maintenance of spiritual and physical strength is important, it is absolutely vital that healthy ways of processing the emotional life of ministry be developed. So many leaders give up because their emotional resilience is lacking or has dried up completely. The kind term given to this distressing state is "burnout."

Burnout in the life of the ministry leader is simply a case of emotional exhaustion.[1.] While exhaustion can sometimes be physical or spiritual, it is often the intense emotional demands of ministry that cause us to stumble or wear out. In saying that, if part of our being is affected, the whole suffers. The insidious nature of emotional depletion is that it sneaks up on us with the point of self-awareness being the moment we crash and burn.

I know of one very gifted pastor who suddenly resigned from his church. From the outside things were going well. It wasn't as if the church was struggling; in fact, it was known to be a very influential ministry. The resignation surprised both his church and his ministry colleagues, who were somewhat perplexed by the decision. Later, the pastor owned up to not being able to handle the occasions when somebody left his church. He took every departure as a personal rejection. His decision to quit, then, was something of an overreaction to a normal process of church life. Any experienced pastor knows that attendance turnover in the church is simply part of the deal. He would have known that too, so what caused him to take that course?

The pastor was most likely carrying within himself a degree of insecurity in identity. This made him vulnerable to personal injury at the emotional level every time someone left the church. Whatever the root cause, it is apparent that the constant pain of people leaving extended far beyond the pastor's emotional capacity to cope. Emotional depletion caused him to lose perspective and to regard the leaving of some as an indication of a broader failure of his ministry. Unable to bear the pain any longer, resignation became the chosen way of escape. The fall of his ministry was caused by a lack of emotional resilience rather than any spiritual or physical cause.

Developing your emotional capacity is so essential to ministry survival that church consultant John Finkelde says, "Pastors must learn to manage their emotional energy more than their time." Obviously, organizing your time wisely is important. His statement does not negate that, but the management of your emotions is far more foundational to your long term survival in ministry. This will mean gaining understanding of where your emotional ceiling lies, recognizing the signs of emotional depletion and knowing the steps required not just for emotional refueling, but also for the enlargement of your capacity.

While the consequences of emotional burnout can be sudden and catastrophic, ironically the warning signs may have been evident for a while. If you find yourself frequently becoming moody, tired, irritable, complaining, and inclined to overreact, you are showing the early signs of emotional drain. Often it will be those closest to you who pick up on it, (usually because they are the first affected by it), while others remain blissfully unaware as you play the pretend game of "coping" to others. The first step in avoiding a decline into total burnout is to humbly listen to those around you. If you don't, you will reach the point of exhaustion where you will lose sight of reality, refuse advice and make irrational decisions that spiral your downfall.

Lessons for when the emotional tank runs dry

The story of the Prophet Elijah's own emotional dive (1 Kings 19) provides some salutary lessons for dealing with this problem. In the first instance we might be surprised to realize that even the most anointed and gifted ministry leaders can succumb. Another interesting fact is that Elijah's emotional battle occurred after a resounding spiritual victory. Both the highs and lows of ministry effort can take their toll. The climbing of any mountain can be followed by a slippery slide into the valley. This was Elijah's experience. After a great display of God's supernatural power through his ministry over the impotent Baal god and the humiliation of the Baal prophets on Mount Carmel, Elijah flees in fear of his life.

Getting as far away from the threat as possible, Elijah retreated alone into the Sinai wilderness, eventually collapsing at the foot of a solitary tree *"and prayed that he might die. 'I have had enough, Lord,' he said. 'Take my life, for I am no better than my ancestors'"* (1 Kings 19:4b). Therein lies the first lesson:

Avoid making big decisions when you are in the desert

Emotional exhaustion is a very vulnerable place to be in. When you are near or over the edge of your emotional capacity, the enemy will have a go at you. Make no mistake. The Devil fights dirty. He knows the time to kick a person is when he is down. The battleground is usually the mind. When you are tired, negative, confusing and contradictory thoughts will assail you. What you think and what you feel are ultimately translated into action. If you do not appreciate the unreliability of your thoughts and feelings in these times, you are liable to make major decisions that turn out to be the wrong ones. It is in moments of extreme emotional depletion that leaders say along with Elijah, "I don't want to do this anymore. I've had enough!" Leaders quit ministries, husbands and wives quit marriages, workers quit jobs, friends quit friendships and members quit churches, only to lament the decision when the trial has passed.

The trouble with important decision making when discouraged is that perceptions are invariably distorted. Problems are blown out of proportion. As a result, the ability to make sound rational decisions is distorted. It is unwise, therefore, to make decisions that will have dramatic ramifications for your future when you are emotionally spent.

Elijah was in exactly that state of mind. He saw himself and his ministry as a failure and felt isolated in his ministry endeavors: *"I alone am left"* (1 Kings 20:10, 14). The Lord later corrected that erroneous view, reminding Elijah that there were in fact *"seven thousand others in Israel who had never bowed to Baal"* (1 Kings 19:18). That is just how it is when your emotional capacity has been drained. Perception is unreliable. Things appear worse than they really are. You are just not in the position to make reliable and rational decisions. So don't even try to go there!

Take time out to be refreshed

Fortunately, God did not respond to Elijah's request to take him out. Instead God dealt with Elijah's predicament in a very pragmatic way:

"Then he lay down and slept under the broom tree. But as he was sleeping, an angel touched him and told him, 'Get up and eat!' He looked around and saw some bread baked on hot stones and a jar of water! So he ate and drank and lay down again" (1 Kings 19:5-6).

Many might offer a more spiritual response to his situation such as, "You just need to press into God more, Elijah" or "pray harder, Elijah." It is interesting to note that God's first action in tending to Elijah was more material than spiritual. What Elijah needed before anything else was simply a good feed and a good sleep!

Have you ever heard the saying, "When it is hardest to pray, that is when you should pray the hardest"? In other words, some intense and prolonged intercession on your part is supposed to do it. Let me tell you that that is an idealistic proposition. From personal experience I have found that when you reach such a low point, there is nothing in you to get past the desperate cry of "Oh God, help me!" Prayer is necessary and important but when you are in that place, you will need others who will stand in the gap for you.

Get some rest! Jesus himself understood the importance of taking moments of "time out" from the exhausting demands of ministry. After Jesus had fed the five thousand and the apostles had completed a ministry tour of the area, Jesus said to them, *"Let us get away from the crowds for a while and rest"* (Mark 6:31). The invitation was not just for the benefit of his disciples but also for his own. His occasions for rest were preventative measures to guard against exhaustion. We can learn from him. His passion for the completion of his mission was far greater than ours, his ministry tenure far shorter than most. It would have been understandable if Jesus had said, "No time for rest, there is work to be done and little time in which to do it." The point is, even the Son of God with the fullness of God in him still in his humanity understood the absolute necessity for time for physical and emotional replenishment.

Prevention is indeed the best cure and if you find yourself having an Elijah experience, chances are you have not been good at this. Physical rest is the first spoonful of medicine when you have bottomed out emotionally. Do whatever you love doing, get away somewhere into the outdoors, the beach or read a good book, even before you try getting into the Bible. Don't let a spiritually pious attitude suggest that this might not be the right order for recovery.

Get alone with God

Only after a time of physical replenishment does Elijah find the strength to carry out a forty day journey to Mount Sinai, the mountain of God. Having been rested and refreshed, his recovery is now one of emotional and spiritual pursuit. Mount Sinai is the place of God's presence and appearance, the place from which he speaks. Elijah makes this journey with a longing to hear from God again. Arriving at the mountain he finds a cave, a place of solitude. Finding a quiet place to be alone with God is imperative for the hearing of his voice.

God starts the conversation with a probing question: *"What are you doing here Elijah?"* (1 Kings 19:9). Of course God already knew. The question was for Elijah's benefit. It was really an invitation: "Open your heart Elijah, talk to me, spill it out!" And out it came. All of Elijah's confusion, frustration and complaint flowed like a river bursting its banks. "How did it come to this? I've been serving my heart out. I've given it my best shot! Why is everything against me? I feel so alone!"

Like a mighty wind, the upheaval of an earthquake and a raging fire, Elijah's emotional turmoil envelops him. Then in a sudden moment of calm, God speaks. The same question is put again, the last dribble of complaint extracted. It was done. It was the catharsis needed, the moment of settling down, of letting go and letting God. In that instance Elijah's spirit is revitalized. He is in the presence of the Lord, close enough and settled enough to hear God whisper. His touch, his fresh word, supernaturally refreshes, empowers and strengthens the emotions and the spirit. Physically, emotionally then spiritually renewed, Elijah is charged to serve again and he rises to complete his ministry.

For most of us the journey of recovery will not be as clear cut or as short as a forty day run across the dessert. I have faced burnout personally. In my thirty years of ministry I have been taken to the edge of my emotional capacity many times. On one occasion I seriously tipped over the precipice. It was a two year sojourn of life reorganizing, soul searching, buckets of tears and God-seeking in the wilderness, before God enabled me to rise again.

Be aware that emotional burnout in ministry leadership is an occupational hazard. It is a trap in the cosmic conflict you are involved in. In his book, *Pastors of Promise,* Jack Hayford reminds the ministry leader, *"Hell has no kind thoughts about you…ever! He wants you out of the way and even at your weakest you are still an annoyance to his counsels."*[2] All church leaders get deeply discouraged and emotionally depleted. You are not alone in your experience. The Devil works hard to cause you to lose heart but, says Hayford, *"Your placement comes from the hand of the Highest. God's word settles the source of your appointment and the sufficiency of your gifting – you are given by Christ and graced by his hand."* [3]

If you do find yourself feeling beaten up, take time out to take care of yourself. Better still, build rest into your schedule before you get run down. Rest up but never give up. God will grace you to overcome! He will empower you afresh to run again, to finish the race, and complete the task he has given you.

End notes:

[1] Brookes R. Faulkerner, *Burnout in Ministry*. Broadman Press 1981, U.S.A., page 40.

[2] Jack Hayford, *Pastors of Promise*. Regal Books, California, U.S.A., 1997, page 228.

[3] Jack Hayford, op.cit., page 22.

Chapter Six
Marriage, Family and Ministry Balance

Without doubt the ministry leadership vocation can be extremely tough on families. A survey in the USA showed that the divorce rate for pastors ranked third after medical doctors and police officers. Even then it was suggested that more ministers would get divorced but stuck with difficult marriages either for theological reasons or out of professional necessity.

Most ministry leaders and pastors will struggle with the ministry and family balance. In my early days in ministry, especially when my children were young, I was not particularly good at this. Too many times I allowed family to be crowded out by ministry concerns.

Every leader should understand how the demands of ministry can deeply impinge. The natural stresses that come along with the spiritual challenges of ministry will expose any weaknesses in the marriage and family relationships. If they exist, the enemy will go for the area of vulnerability every time. It fact, it can be expected that the adversary will attempt to direct spiritual attack at the family of the leader.

While it is unreasonable to suggest the leader must have the perfect family, it is important that things are relatively strong and stable relationally. If the family is not doing well, it is a certainty that the leader will not be doing well. Conflict on the home front will have its effect on the leader's ministry effectiveness. It may ultimately undermine his credibility. The apostle Paul alludes to the necessity of the leader's family being in order, saying, *"He must manage his own family well, with children who respect and obey him. For if a man cannot manage his own household, how can he take care of God's church?"* (1 Timothy 3:4-5).

A good family environment and a good ministry are somewhat dependent upon each other. They are not mutually exclusive in the marriage, family and ministry partnership. Bearing this in mind, the leader should commit to the family's care and well-being as much as he might to his ministry. Marriage and family skills are important because they are the most important relationships outside of your relationship with God.[1] It is important to develop healthy ways of open and direct communication with your spouse around time management, finances, parenting, and other issues that integrate with the pressures of ministry.

The question of ministry versus marriage and family is really a matter of setting right priorities. While at times the family may make sacrifices for ministry, I do not believe God calls us to sacrifice family for the sake of ministry. It is incumbent on the leader to manage things lovingly and competently enough to show that family truly comes first and the ministry second. The family should never play second fiddle to ministry. The following guidelines, learned out of my own shortcomings in this area, will help negotiate the pitfalls and keep your marriage, family and ministry safe.

Being there

I can recall times when I have been at home with family in body but not in mind and spirit, with my heart and thoughts preoccupied with ministry matters. This disengagement is keenly felt by those dear to you who at times want your undivided attention. If you have difficultly switching off, a conscious effort needs to be made to focus on personal family attentiveness and interaction. If you don't do this, resentment will build up in the hearts of those who need you. Being there in reality, not virtual reality, is paramount.

As far as possible be there for what is important to family, e.g., birthdays, wedding anniversaries, the parent-teacher meetings, the prize givings and the kids' sports games. To miss these family moments for some less than vitally important ministry demand can work detrimentally on the health of family life. Some things missed will leave you with regret. One of the dumbest things I did was to miss my father's 80th birthday (albeit in another city) because I had committed to do a wedding for a couple I hardly knew and whom I have never seen again. Right there is a prime example of the misplaced sense of priority of ministry over family.

Being there includes blocking out your calendar for holidays and quality time (which also means quantity time) with your spouse and family. Then you need to resist the temptation to make adjustments because of ministry demands that arise. Many leaders (especially pastors) find themselves not taking the vacation time due to them, losing precious opportunity to spend time with family to the tyranny of ministry busyness.

Guard against ministry home invasion

As far as possible, try to make the home something of a sanctuary from the tensions and pressures of ministry. Those who have ever had to work from a home office will appreciate how difficult that can be! If you are in that situation, the best thing you can do is to get an office somewhere else! Even when the office is outside of the home, be aware ministry will try to follow you home, imposing itself like an uninvited guest.

It pays to put in place some strategies to protect your family life. Simple things like keeping "after hours" business meetings out of the home, switching off the cell phone, a voice mailbox for your landline, and avoiding after-hours checks of the work e-mail, are smart ideas. Evening mealtimes and the period before the kids go to bed should be exclusively for family. Don't set a place at the table for ministry matters. Nothing short of a life and death situation should be allowed to intrude.

One of the best things you can do to guard against ministry home invasion is to protect your family from exposure to the negative and frustrating aspects of leadership. This means watching your attitudes and your conversation.

The challenge around this is protecting the family as much as you can from the criticism that can be directed against you. As difficult as this might be, try not to expose them to harm by processing the hurt you might be feeling over a ministry matter with them or in front of them. If you are being attacked or let down in some way, they will feel it personally too. Be aware that spouses and children can easily get "drawn into the vortex" of crushing criticism to the point that they are often radically and emotionally scarred and permanently discouraged from enthusiasm for loving any future service in churches.[2] My eldest son, once commented, *"Dad, I would never want to be a pastor!"* That is a sad indictment on my inability to protect him when he was younger from the harsh pummeling ministry leadership can sometimes bring.

There does of course need to be an outlet for the disappointments of ministry leadership. But constantly using your spouse as the dumping ground (especially when the kids are within earshot) will not help for a happy home atmosphere or view of ministry life.

Be mutually supportive of each other's role

It is crucial that each spouse share the call to ministry leadership. It is never going to work if one spouse is not "feeling it," or worse still, resisting it. One of the essential signs of the right timing for release into a call to ministry leadership is that both husband and wife will be in agreement.

Once in agreement, each should also be supportive and respectful of the nature of each other's role. Both should be able to clearly define what those roles are and how they fit together in a complimentary sense. This does not mean that both husband and wife should share equal leadership responsibility or involvement. What it does mean is that there must be an explicit understanding and agreement about each other's contribution. Where a husband and wife share equally in leadership over a ministry, it is still necessary to determine who will be the "senior" in the partnership. There can be only one captain on the ship's bridge. While co-leaders function as a partnership, understanding the boundaries for individual and collective decision making is vital.

In many cases it is just one partner who carries the bulk of the leadership burden while the other contributes primarily with home and/or financial support. While one is immersed in ministry, the other has to keep the home fires burning or "bring home the bacon." I recall the days when my own wife did exactly that. I used to complain that she should do more in the church – as if full time work, three kids, managing the home and being a superb hostess wasn't enough! God later showed me that what she did was essential to the ministry. If she hadn't done what she did, I wouldn't have been able to do what I did. As I reflect, I am so extremely thankful for her support and enduring ability to live with all the implications that went with a church planting call.

Ultimately, "who does what" in the leader partnership should be determined by God given desires and gifting. It will also be set by the different stages of life and seasons in marriage and family. Understanding and flexibility are the key.

End notes:

[1]Alexander Venter, *Doing Church*. Vineyard International Publishing, Cape Town, South Africa, 2000, page 185.

[2]Dr, John Gilmore, *Pastoral Politics, Why Ministers Resign*. AMG Publishers 2002, page 178.

Chapter Seven
Faith for the Journey

Faith is the absolute prerequisite for anything God will do. It is the key to the inheritance of God's promises to us for life and ministry. I am so thankful that God has placed me in a church movement that carries within its DNA a "positive faith attitude." This kind of faith exudes by example from the C3 Church's president and founder Pastor Phil Pringle. This great leader carries the gift of faith in such a way that it spills over to ignite the hearts of others. Whether you sit under his teaching at a conference or engage in a casual conversation over a coffee, you will be inspired to believe in God for the fulfillment of a far bigger dream. If you want to be encouraged, Pastor Phil has written extensively on the subject. His book, simply entitled *Faith*[1] should be in every ministry leader's library.

In Hebrews 11:1 the question, *"What is faith?"* is followed immediately by the answer: *"It is the confident assurance that what we hope for is going to happen. It is the evidence of things we cannot see."* As a young Christian, I used a printed but succinct presentation of the gospel to help me share Christ. At the end of the script I remember the statement, *"You have received Christ by faith not feelings."* On reflection I think it was there as an indemnity, just in case no one actually "felt" anything after praying. If there was no awareness of God's touch in the moment, the assurance was given: "Well, you asked him [Jesus] in, so he is there by faith, no matter what you feel."

It is true that feelings or the lack of them may not be a reliable indicator of anything. However, in my personal experience and observations, genuine faith sooner or later reveals itself by an internal subjective presence. This is the "confident assurance" or the "evidence" referred to in Hebrew 11:1. In other words, faith is a feeling; it is an attitude you can have within you.[2]

A few years ago I had the privilege of attending Pastor Yongi Cho's Church Growth Conference in Seoul. I had the chance to spend an hour or so in one of the prayer cubicles at Prayer Mountain. Among other things, I was seeking God for the growth of the church up to five hundred (we were stuck on about four hundred). I was frustrated at the lack of breakthrough. We were doing all the right things. The worship services had God's presence. The leadership structure and systems were all in place for a push forward but we were not seeing the increase. As I set this before God I felt the Holy Spirit say, *"Five hundred! That's easy for me."* In that instant what seemed to be something of a difficulty became a possibility. The "feeling" just dropped on me. When I arrived back in New Zealand, the moment the plane landed I knew something had changed. Everything seemed smaller: the airport terminal, the city, the church building. This was partly a matter of perspective compared to the largeness of things in Seoul. But it was also something else. I could *"feel"* that a church of five hundred was totally achievable. In my heart I knew it would happen. From that day things broke open, and the church soared to over five hundred in one year. Nothing was done differently. The only change was in me. It wasn't that things were smaller, really; it was just that I had gotten bigger on the inside. Faith does that. It changes your perspective on things.

The best way I can describe faith is as an absolute, unshakable "*knowing*" that what God has promised by his Spirit will become a reality in the natural world. Faith is an attitude, however else we may describe it. So is faith's opposite, *"unbelief."* We all know the feelings that are characteristic of a lack of faith, i.e., doubt, cynicism, fear, uncertainty, and anxiety. To try and divorce faith from feeling doesn't make sense. If I am not feeling it, I probably don't have it!

It was the lack of faith that initially kept Israel out of the land promised to them. Again, perspective was an issue. Their negative perception became their reality. In their unbelief and up against the giants of Canaan, Israel *"felt like grasshoppers next to them"* (Numbers 14:13).

Since faith is always the key that unlocks God's promises to you, the enemy will do all he can to rob you of it. He will constantly seek to undermine your God given vision and impede your progress towards it. The fiery darts of doubt will bombard you constantly. Disappointments, failed expectations, rejections, long delays and other challenges can serve to erode your faith if you allow it. The enemy wants you to have the attitude of "I can't" rather than "I can." That kind of thinking always diminishes your view of yourself and your view of what is possible with God. Given the intensity of the fight, you must develop ways of replenishing faith in order to push through and realize your dreams.

How much faith do I need and where do I get it from?

When Peter began to sink after an initial surge of faith which enabled him to walk on water, Jesus said to him, *"You of little faith, why did you doubt?"* (Matthew 14:31). Jesus on several occasions admonished the disciples for a lack of faith with these words. Our perception then is that faith is a matter of size. We often think of someone having great faith or little faith. However, to think of faith in terms of "how much" comes unstuck when we consider that Jesus also said:

"I assure you, even if you had faith as small as a mustard seed, you could say to this mountain, 'Move from here to there' and it would move. Nothing would be impossible" (Matthew 17:20). Clearly faith is not something that is to be measured in quantity. So what did Jesus mean when he said Peter had *"little faith"*?

The clue is given by what Jesus *did* even before he *spoke.* As Peter began to sink under the waves he cried out, *"Lord save me!" Immediately Jesus reached out his hand and caught him"* (Matthew 14:30-31). What happened next? I can't imagine that Jesus heaved Peter over his shoulder and carried him back to the boat. My guess is that they walked together on the water, Peter's hand in his. Peter's miraculous experience only faltered when he took his eyes off Jesus. His focus shifted to the wind and seas raging about him. In that instant he lost the confident assurance that faith brings. In response to his cry for help, Jesus then reaches out his hand and catches him. Right there we are taught something about faith. Faith has nothing to do with size but everything to do with connection with Jesus. Little faith is the same as little connection. Little faith is not small in quantity; it is small in quality. Weak faith in any moment is a consequence of a weak connection with Christ in that moment.

Your degree of faith is dependent on your degree of intimacy in relationship with Jesus. Paul tells us that *"faith comes from hearing the message, and the message is heard through the word of Christ"* (Romans 10:19). Hearing is important for stimulating faith but we can only hear the word of Christ when we are close to him. If we are dull to hearing his voice then it is likely we are distracted and distanced from him.

Failure to pursue our relationship with Christ inevitably results in an attitude of God forgetfulness. This leads to self reliance and the erosion of faith under the constant bombardment of doubts hurled at you by the enemy. This is a barren place to live. Faith is to be constantly cultivated and replenished. It is something that can grow, perhaps not in size but certainly in quality. It comes from and is strengthened by a sustained connection with the Lord Jesus Christ.

The fight to maintain faith

Think thoughts of faith

Faith has application in every area of our spiritual journey. This discussion on the subject is centered around the pursuit of faith to complete your ministry call.

Growing and maintaining the place of faith is very much a fight. Throughout the process of developing faith, doubts around the promises of God will repeatedly try to prevent you from gaining ground. Doubts will also try to take back the ground you have already conquered. I say this so that you are not fazed by moments when the assault comes. Paul is our model. Nearing the end of his life and ministry, he triumphantly declares, *"I have fought a good fight, I have finished the race, and I have remained faithful"* (2 Timothy 4:8). Despite the constant and sometimes ferocious attacks Paul faced in his ministry, he fought the mind games and won the battle. He stayed in faith and stayed the course. He saw things through to the finish. He "remained faithful" or "full of faith" and this gave him his staying power.

The battleground for faith verses doubt takes place in the mind. I believe it was in the mind that Paul won the fight for faith every time. He disciplined himself to *"think about things that are pure and lovely and admirable"* and to *"think about things that are excellent and worthy of praise"* (Philippians 4:8). He knew the key was to "*guard heart and mind*" [from wrong thinking] "*as you live in Jesus*" (Philippians 4:7). That's why staying close to Christ is necessary. By hearing his word, his thoughts become your thoughts. The power of his word permeates your mind and transforms the way you think. That same power ultimately enables you to accomplish things.

It may surprise you to know that even Abraham, one of the greatest examples of a life lived by faith, had to deal with the matter of doubt. It's right there in the Bible! When God promised this elderly patriarch and his hitherto barren and now beyond child bearing age wife, Sarah, that they would have a son, *"he laughed to himself in disbelief"* (Genesis 17:17). Sarah also *"laughed silently to herself"* (Genesis 18:12) at the seeming impossibility of God's promise. To top it off, this doubting duo sought to cover up their disbelief. Abraham bowed down in worship hiding a questioning heart. Sarah denied (to the Lord himself) that she had even scoffed at his promise. God had spoken, and straight away the enemy sought to snatch the promise from their hands. The struggle for faith against doubt had begun. It was internal. It was a battle inside the mind.

Despite this conflict in which doubt appeared to have the upper hand, something shifted over time. It is later said of Abraham:

"When God promised Abraham that he would become the father of many nations, Abraham believed him" (Romans 4:18).

"And Abraham's faith did not weaken, even though he was too old to be a father at the age of one hundred and that Sarah, his wife, had never been able to have children" (Romans 4:19)

At first these texts appear to contradict the Genesis record. Instead, they tell the story of Abraham's victory of faith over doubt. When the promise was given, Abraham's faith was nearly as weak as it could get. The promise was too impossible for him to believe. However, as Abraham journeyed with God, he stayed close and meditated on the promise in his mind. Then the reliability and certainty of God's words took hold. From the beginning it was a matter of decision: the decision about which voice he would allow to dominate his thinking. He chose the voice of faith. Doubt was overcome; *"In fact, his faith grew stronger, and in this he brought glory to God"* (Romans 4:20).

The interesting thing is that Abraham's faith was able to grow in strength and quality so that it was impervious to the voice of unbelief. Growth requires time and nurture. This requires a disciplined focus in your thinking on what God has spoken and a submitting of your mind to his truth. The enemy will hit you with negative thinking continually. Don't listen to the voices that will discourage your faith. Don't measure the promises against the present circumstances. Think only in terms of what God has said to you. Negative thinking will keep you out of the promise, but a positive faith attitude will usher you in. Let God's word fill the sanctuary of your mind.

Speak words of faith

Positive faith thinking results in positive faith speaking. What you feel on the inside always spills out of the mouth. It just happens that way. You can tell when someone carries a positive faith attitude. It is reflected in the way they speak. Caleb is my positive "faith speak" hero. One of the twelve spies sent in by Moses to reconnoiter the Promised Land before Israel was to make its big entry, Caleb (along with Joshua) soundly undercut the cries of the other ten spies. Amidst the vociferous negative cries of, *"the land is full of giants, the fortresses are too strong, we can't do this,"* Caleb makes an emphatic faith statement *"Certainly we can do it!"* (Numbers 13:30). Unfortunately, Caleb's cry of faith was swamped in a sea of fear as the bigger crowd caved in to the spies' unbelief. The promise was missed by a whole generation. Negativity is like that. Give it a platform and it spreads like influenza!

If you want to build something, "certainly we can do it" people are the best people to have on your team. As leaders we should be that kind of person. I am not talking about those who speak out of a confidence in their own ability, but those who speak out of their trust in God. I'm not suggesting that we should ignore the realities of the challenges to overcome in order to get to the promise. But we should be counted among those who believe that when God leads us to do something then he will be with us to enable it to be done.

I once took over a church that was led by a very nice but ineffective board who were used to collectively making the leadership decisions. The problem was they were so cautious about everything they never seemed to be able to make one. Because I was feeling my way, I was somewhat tentative in exercising a more confident leadership role. My ministry background was in a denomination where the pastor served with an elected team and everything was voted on. I was needing to learn some things about leadership. After a few months of frustration and listening to an avalanche of negative reasons why a particular project I had submitted that meeting could not be done, I halted the discussion with an exasperated plea:

"Stop! Guys, please don't tell me why it can't be done. Tell me how it can be done!" After a stunned silence the focus of the rhetoric changed to how things could in fact happen. And they did – happen, that is! They actually got excited as solution after solution rolled off their tongues.

That's what happens when you shift your language to how it *"can be"* done instead of it *"can't be."* I think the positive thinking and speaking crowd have locked on to something powerful. They understand the power of confession, albeit somewhat limited, compared with the power of speaking what God has spoken. There is an old saying, *"Where there is a will there is a way."* If that applies at the human level, how much more it applies when we are doing God's will. He will always make a way. As leaders, our conversation should always reflect our faith in his promises in positive and confident language. Whatever the circumstances are saying, seek to stay in positive faith and speak life. Be a "Caleb" kind of leader who is "a can do" kind of person.

Do acts of faith

Genuine faith means that thoughts and words will always be congruent. It is easy to speak apparent words of faith while hiding unbelief in the heart. James highlights this inconsistency saying, *"What's the use of saying you have faith if you don't prove it by your actions"* (James 2:4). Professed faith that is not followed by action is not faith at all. It is just big talk! Real faith will always lead us to a personal obedient response to that which God has spoken. We will take the pragmatic steps we need to take in order to enter into the promise.

Most often when we are required to take the first step of faith, the circumstances may not be quite right, the timing may seem inconvenient, the resources may not be all together and the obstacles may loom large before you. A voice shouts loudly at this point, *"Not yet! Wait for things to fall into place!"* Inaction is the usual result. Waiting for more favorable circumstances before stepping out might seem to be the right thing to do from our perspective. It makes sense.

Having things make sense is an important consideration, except in matters of faith. Common sense would say Noah was crazy to build an ark, Abraham was unwise leaving home not knowing where he was going and Simon Peter and his partners were foolish to throw in their fishing business to follow an itinerant religious teacher.

To be fair, common sense can be an acceptable and justifiable excuse not to act. On the other hand it might be just plain disobedience. Disobedience is the fruit of a lack of genuine faith. At times and especially at the start of fulfilling a ministry leadership call, action outside of the comfortable boundaries of normal sensibility is required. To stumble at this point, at the starting blocks, is to lose the race even before it begins.

In my experience God looks to us to be obedient in action before things actually begin to fall into place. Look at Israel's second opportunity to enter into Canaan. The tests of faith were all still there: the giant enemy warriors, the fortresses, and the added inconvenience of the River Jordan in flood. Common sense leadership would say, "The timing is not right! Let's at least wait until the waters have receded!"

This time though, only one voice spoke and that was the voice of faith. *"Then Joshua told the people, 'Purify yourselves, for tomorrow the Lord will do great wonders among you...' Think of it! The Ark of the Covenant, which belongs to the Lord of the whole earth, will lead you across the River Jordan"* (Joshua 3:5, 11).

With an unbelieving generation now gone, a faith filled generation acted according to the word. *"'The priests will be carrying the Ark of the Lord, the Lord of all the earth. When their feet touch the water the flow of water will be cut off upstream'...the priests who were carrying the Ark of the Lord's Covenant stood on dry ground in the middle of the riverbed as the people passed by them. They waited there until everyone had crossed on dry ground"* (Joshua 3:13, 17).

The important thing to note is that this act of faith was not contingent on timing or circumstances being right. I can't imagine what was going on in the minds of the leaders of this desert raised nonswimmer generation as they headed towards deep water. The thoughts "*I can't walk on water, I can't breathe underwater*" or *"I can't swim"* were obviously suppressed by an unshakable, dominant faith, willing to act.

There is this certain recklessness about great steps of faith. It is about being willing to get in over our heads. John Wimber said faith (from our perspective) is spelled r-i-s-k. Real faith steps out, despite the barriers. It pushes beyond acceptable or comfortable levels.

As Israel took the first step, God acted in response to that faith. God then caused circumstances to fall into place. That is the secret to the miraculous. So often we wait for God to act, when God is waiting for us to act. When we move in faith, he moves in power.

Faith is action. Believe God. Think it, speak it and make an effort; be a doer. Faith pleases God and brings his reward. When faith acts it will cause you to rise higher then you ever thought, take you further than you ever dreamed and exceed all the expectations you ever had.

End notes:

[1] Dr Phil Pringle, *Faith*. Pax Trading Ministries Pty Limited, Sydney, Australia, 1991, page 19.

[2] Dr Phil Pringle, op.cit.

Chapter Eight
Developing a Right View of Ministry Success

One of the big frustrations causing a leader to throw in the towel is a perceived lack of ministry success. There is nothing worse than feeling that despite all of your hard, sacrificial work, your expectations are not being realized. There are two aspects that govern our view of success: the time frame in which things happen, and how we measure it.

The matter of time frame is more readily understood. There are exceptions but things usually don't happen overnight. We all appreciate that the future viability of most ministries depends on a solid foundation being laid. It is always the foundational work that takes the longest. If you are not prepared to do the hard yards for the long haul, you will soon become disappointed. The Christian life and ministry is about the journey. Perseverance is essential. Paul reiterates this, saying, *"So don't get tired of doing what is good. Don't get discouraged and give up, for we will reap a harvest of blessing at the appropriate time"* (Gal 6:9).

Waiting for the breakthrough is a great test. In an age of instant gratification, impatience for the reward is a common saboteur of ultimate ministry success. So many quit, thinking they are at the edge of their limits when in fact they are at the edge of their breakthrough. What might have been the outcome for Israel if they had stopped their march around the city of Jericho at lap number six? Don't be fooled into thinking failure just because success is not happening according to your timetable. God has his timing. The promise will come in time, at the right time, so don't be tempted to quit before that time. Breakthrough might be waiting for you, after one more march around Jericho!

Quantity versus quality

Success in ministry is often viewed from a somewhat worldly perspective, being very much gauged by size and numbers. The first question after worship services and events is "How many?" When numbers are deemed the primary measurement for success, the leaders of larger churches are deemed to "have it" while the leaders of smaller churches "have not." This idea can lead to a sense of competition among pastors and with it an internal pressure to make the church grow. This is acutely felt if your sense of identity and worth is dependent on this perception of success, or if your subliminal goal is for esteem and recognition from others.

The old adage "size matters" is alive and well in the church. When pastors get together the question on their hearts, if not on their lips, is "How big is yours?" It's amazing how many pastors exaggerate the answer to that question. Undoubtedly, the size of a church or ministry is an indicator of something, but is size alone really the indicator of success or not? Many would seem to think so given the focus on quantitative growth goals and the priority given to making the numbers. Setting numerical goals is important. It is not wrong in itself, but should it be the driving priority?

The first goal of ministry leadership, especially in the church, is outlined clearly in Ephesians 4:12-13: *"Their responsibility is to equip God's people to do his work and build up the church, the body of Christ, until we come to such unity in our faith and knowledge of God's Son that we will be mature and full grown in the Lord, measuring up to the full stature of Christ."*

However many people God has entrusted to us, the first priority is always the spiritual maturity of those we lead. Quality more than quantity should be our concern. It is out of quality that quantity comes. A well planted and nurtured tree will always produce the most fruit. In the normal course of church life we can expect quality to bring forth quantity, as that life reproduces itself. Quantity is not the goal; quality is.

The fact is, though, that it is possible to produce quantity without spiritual quality. Eugene Peterson, in reference to the church in his country, warns:

"The pastors of America have metamorphosed into a company of shopkeepers and the shops they keep are churches. They are preoccupied with shopkeeper's concerns – how to keep the customers happy, how to lure customers away from competition...how to package the goods so that the customer will lay out more money."[1]

This is hard hitting but valid criticism. There is a tendency in parts of the church to pander to the consumer mindset of our culture. We strive to present the best product in order to attract the biggest crowd. To grow a large church you don't have to be a spiritually gifted pastor; you just need to be a good shopkeeper, a good salesman or businessman.

Of course, we all want our church or ministry to grow but it should not be at the expense of the critical role of leadership, which is to provide spiritual nurture and direction. We should not give ourselves to "the idolatry of numbers and the idea that our success is based on how large the church is."[2] Our call is to lead our people to maturity in Christ. One pertinent question to ask more often is not "How many?" but "How did this event help people towards a deeper relationship with Christ?"[3]

How should ministry success be defined?

There is no doubt that when Jesus calls us to a purpose he calls us to success, not failure. Jesus said, *"My true disciples produce much fruit. This brings glory to the Father"* (John 15:8). "Much fruit" metaphorically describes abundant productivity resulting from what we do. The word "fruit" is translated from the Greek word "karpos" which according to Strongs refers to fruit [as plucked] literally or figuratively. [4]

The use of the word "karpos" in other places in Scripture gives some idea as to what Jesus had in mind. Fruit is defined as:

Spiritual maturity evidenced in character

"...he will produce this kind of ***fruit*** *in us; love, joy, peace, patience, kindness, goodness, faithfulness, gentleness and self control"* (Galatians 5:22 NLT).

Speaking praise to God

"By him therefore let us offer the sacrifice of praise to God continually, that is, the ***fruit*** *of our lips, giving thanks to his name"* (Hebrews 13:15 KJV).

Goodness of heart shown by good deeds

"But the wisdom that is from above is first pure, then peaceable, gentle and easy to be entreated, full of mercy and good ***fruits****, without partiality, and without hypocrisy. And the* ***fruit*** *of righteousness is sown in peace of them that make peace"* (James 3:17-18 KJV).

Generous giving to those in need

"When I have sealed to them this ***fruit*** [a financial gift to the poor in the church at Jerusalem] *I will come by you into Spain"* (Romans 15:28 KJV).

Serving Christ in the building of his church

"...if I live , that means ***fruitful*** *service for Christ"* (Philippians 1:22).

Reaching others for Christ

"...often I purposed to come unto you...that I might have some ***fruit*** *among you also, even as among other Gentiles"* (Romans 1:13).

Whatever interpretation we give to the term "much fruit," it is clear that it relates to all that truly represents or reproduces Christ in some way. Genuine ministry success is when we see an increasing expression of Christ in all of the above areas flowing out of our work. When Christ is revealed in all that we produce and develop in our lives and in the lives of others, the Father is given glory. The glory is not for ourselves as we deem ourselves to be successful. The glory is towards the Father as we succeed in making Christ known, because the glory of the Father is seen in the Son.

How big the numbers, the building or the salary are merely superficial indicators of success. Success is far better defined by the degree of overall impact a church has *for* Christ, arising from the quality of its life *in* Christ, irrespective of more worldly barometers.

John Bevere makes the point, *"There are large churches that lack influence in their communities and, conversely, there are small churches that are very influential. The important aspect of an effective church is not numeric but the quality of their outreach and influence."*[5] In other words, success is better defined by how much Christ's character, life and love are being reflected relationally both inside and outside of the church.

Knowing your boundaries

One of the biggest reasons for giving up is the idea that you are not being successful in achieving your goals and expectations. This idea leads to great discouragement and unending frustration. Frustration itself can be your friend. It keeps you from complacency and spurs you to advance. However, if your idea of success is based on the wrong premise, your frustration and disappointment become a setup for a bailout. It is not just the concept of success that is the problem. It is where your expectations of success lie.

When measuring our success or lack of it, the worst thing we can do is compare ourselves with those we think of as doing better. The act of comparison can enhance the feelings of inadequacy and failure. This trap can be avoided if we understand this truth: God does not grant everyone the same! If we cannot accept this, we will be relentlessly driven by unrealistic and unobtainable goals. We are all uniquely equipped for a purpose. What God has called and gifted us to do will have its boundaries according to his plans.

Your degree of potential influence, which includes the size of your church or ministry, will determined by three factors:

1. **Your call** – the specific purpose you are to fulfill

2. **Your capacity** – the specific power (anointing) given to fulfill the call
3. **Your context** – the specific place where the call is to be fulfilled

Call, capacity and context fit together to set your ultimate destiny. To obtain success, it is vital to seek God for a revelation of those boundaries and aim to reach them. Psalm 16:6 reminds us that our boundaries are *"set in pleasant places."* In this respect, never settle for less. Most of us need to push the boundaries of the limitations of our own minds. God doesn't want you to settle for mediocrity. He wants you to experience his favor, to thrive and be an influence beyond the ordinary. His grace is there for your blessing, enjoyment and fulfillment within the parameters of his will which is *"good, pleasing and perfect..."* (Romans 12:2).

At the same time, don't pursue an exaggerated vision beyond God's boundaries for you. Even the great apostle Paul understood this principle: *"But we will not boast of authority we do not have. Our goal is to stay within the boundaries of God's plan for us, and this includes our working there with you"* (2 Corinthians 10:13). Paul knew what he was graced to do and what he was not graced to do! If you know this, you are immediately released from the need to compare yourself with others.

All of us are called and gifted for ministry significance, but not all are called and gifted to ministry prominence. Whatever you do, the goal is to reach your fullest potential bearing the kind of fruit that will glorify God. Pastor Phil Pringle says, *"If you are doing what God wants you to do, you are doing a great thing. It doesn't matter if your church is twenty-five or 25,000!"*

Understanding this, a pastor can base his perception of ministry success not on how big the church is but on how the church is progressing in influence. Is it moving towards its God-given potential for Kingdom impact proportionate to my call, capacity and context? Am I pursuing a vision within the boundaries of what God wants? Are the people entrusted into my care growing in spiritual maturity and finding their own destinies in God? In the end, success is knowing that you have done what God has asked you to do. Success is arriving at the finish line to hear these words of Jesus, "*Well done, my good and faithful servant*" (Matthew 25:21).

End Notes:

[1] Eugene H Peterson, *Working the Angles, The Shape of Pastoral Integrity.* Wm. B. Erdmans Publishing Co., 1987.

[2] Peter Scazzero, Emotional Stability, Leadership Journal, www.christianitytoday.com/le/2012/summer/emotionalstability.html

[3] Greg L Hawkins and Cally Parkinson, *Reveal, Where are you?* Willow, page 68.

[4] James Strong, Strong's Exhaustive Concordance of the Bible.

[5] John Bevere, *Relentless, The Power You Need to Never Give Up.* Waterbook Press, Colorado Springs, Colorado, USA 2011, page 13.

Chapter Nine
The Importance of a Mentor

I took on my first senior leadership of a church at the age of thirty-eight. The opportunity opened up somewhat unexpectedly. The senior pastor of the church had asked me to consider a position as his associate. I was still giving this consideration when he unexpectedly resigned. A few months later I was offered the primary leadership role. At the time, I was regional youth director for the denomination I was with. All my previous local church ministry was as an assistant. This was new territory for me but there was no doubt in my mind that this was a door opened by God. It was a daunting prospective. But then it always is when God asks you to do something related to your call and purpose.

The first couple of years were extremely fruitful as the church embraced a current global charismatic wave of the Holy Spirit and a vision that included church planting and missions. There was significant quantitative growth, much of it coming from salvations supported by solid discipleship ministry taking place within small groups which met in homes. The church was doing great considering its senior pastor was something of a novice.

Many years later as I reflect on that heady start, I realize that it was more than just the euphoria of a "honeymoon" period that set the environment for God to give momentum and increase. It was more subtle than that. God had placed alongside me an older, wiser, spiritual father who without me realizing it at the time, became my mentor.

Fred Wallace, thirty years my senior, the original planter of the church and a long serving elder, stood with me in those initial years as my associate pastor. With that historical pedigree, you might think Fred carried a paternal sense of responsibility for the church but there was never a hint of a desire to control. A man of great love and integrity, Fred always very gently guided me in every important decision. He gave his opinion only when I sought it. He always encouraged me to take new steps of faith, and affirmed or suggested corrections to new ideas I had. He backed me at board meetings, and he gave insight on negotiating difficult conversations and difficult people. He loved me enough to let me learn from my own experiences when I insisted that my way was the best way. He never said "I told you so," if things didn't work out the way I expected. He encouraged me in every sense.

His wife Carole, lovingly supported my wife Wendy, in a similar manner. We had many meals, and we holidayed together. At the heart of the relationship was friendship. The friendship still endures today. Fred is now ninety-three years old! John Kirkpatrick, in his book, *The Power of Mentoring*, regards friendship as the consequential aspect of Christian mentoring: "To know people who think and feel with us, although distant at times," and who "are close to us in spirit, is a priceless asset."[1]

This stability provided to my ministry leadership by Fred's mentoring was not really apparent to me until he decided the day had come for him to retire and step back. There was no reason why the mentoring relationship shouldn't have continued. It didn't because I no longer pursued it. At forty years old I had "come of age" as a leader. I thought I knew enough and thought I knew everything. Such arrogance is not conducive to staying a learner. Someone once said, "Experience teaches fools." It is true that without actual experience, nothing is really learned. However, it is better to learn from someone else's mistakes, and the wisdom learned from these, than to make your own. Suffice to say, in the few years of really flying solo that followed, I learned a lot of lessons the hard way – sometimes at great cost and pain!

Therein lies the benefits of having a mentor. To have someone who has "been there done that" as a model advisor and supporter is invaluable. Many pitfalls can be avoided. Lessons can be learned without the experience of costly mistakes. If mistakes are made or intense challenges are faced, the objective guidance of a mentor will help you negotiate them.

Doing life and ministry with Fred has left a deep impression in me about the need for all developing leaders to have a mentor. The word mentor originated in the Greek story *The Odyssey,* thought to be written by Homer around 750 BC. In that story Odysseus joins the Greek army to fight in the Trojan War. Before leaving his family he appoints his friend Mentor to act as a guide to his son, Telemachus. Over the centuries that followed, "mentor" came to be used to describe those who were influential teachers, tutors and guides.[2]

Another term for mentor is "coach." Everyone understands the importance, necessity and benefits of a sports coach or a business coach. In today's secular world you can even employ a personal life coach if you want one (and can pay for it). While you won't find the word "mentor" in the Bible, coaching or mentoring is a clear Biblical concept. It is the process we call "making disciples."

Jesus commanded his disciples to *"Go and make disciples"* (Matthew 28:19). That means every Christian is to fulfill a mentoring role to some degree. As we follow and serve Christ, we are to model, lead, guide and encourage others who walk with us or come after us on the journey. The basis of discipleship is relationship. The forum for discipleship is the church. All of us need the support, guidance and encouragement of those alongside us or ahead of us on the journey. We need those who are more mature to show the way forward to help us reach our fullest potential in achieving spiritual, personal and professional goals. Mentoring facilitates the growth of another.

Ministry leaders in particular should understand the principle of mentoring and set the goal of reproducing themselves. It is only the secure leader who can do this effectively. To give yourself away and invest in someone who may (hopefully) exceed your own accomplishments will require a personal sense of significance and confidence. You must be free on the inside to invest in others and see them advance. This itself is a personal growth project, but it also means that our contribution towards helping others progress, should increase with our own years and experience.

The purpose of this book is that it will help "mentor" ministry leaders. My desire is that it will enable you to grow in leadership and especially that it might provide you with insight, enabling you to stay the course long term. I am passing on what I have learned from experience, so that you don't have to experience in order to learn. If you do, you can interpret the experience in a way that will help you survive. As you do (survive, that is), you in turn will grow to become an effective mentor.

A lack of mentors for ministry leaders is a challenge faced in the church today. There are very few who have sustained longevity in ministry leadership to pass on their wisdom and experience. Paul suggests a similar situation in the church at Corinth:

"Even though you have ten thousand guardians in Christ, you do not have many fathers, for I became your father through the gospel. Therefore I urge you to imitate me. For this reason I am sending you Timothy, my son, whom I love, who is faithful in the Lord. He will remind you of my way of life in Christ Jesus" (1 Corinthians 4:14-17 NIV).

The word translated as "guardian" refers to a tutor or instructor entrusted with the task of educating the children on behalf of the father. The modern equivalent might be a "nanny" or a schoolteacher. While this is a common type of mentoring, there is a deeper, more meaningful mentoring relationship, one that carries great authority and influence: the "father and son" relationship. Timothy is Paul's spiritual son. The mentoring relationship Paul had with Timothy was life-changing. Timothy modeled aspects of Paul's life so much that his presence at Corinth would be their example to follow, as if Paul himself were there. It is not that Timothy was a clone of Paul. Mentoring is not about control. It is not about seeking to live vicariously through someone else. It is about developing the gifts of another, encouraging and releasing them to be and do their best. A mentor coaches another out of his own personal experience to help that person reach his or her aspirations. However, just as a biological son carries the likeness of the father, Timothy displayed within his own personality and gifts the influence of Paul's mentoring. You, being mentored, will likewise catch the traits of the one mentoring you.

This deeper "father to son" mentoring relationship is invaluable because its foundation is that of love. It is love that motivates the father to pass on all that is helpful to the son so that he reaches his fullest potential. It is that love that allows the son to accept and respond to the corrective guidance of the father. The son knows that the father has only the son's well-being at heart.

The willingness to be mentored

Elijah's mentoring of Elisha is an another example of the "father to son" mentoring relationship. Elisha stuck to Elijah like glue in order to catch what he had: *"As surely as the Lord lives and you yourself live. I will never leave you"* (2 Kings 2:6). When Elijah was suddenly taken up into heaven, Elisha cried out, *"My father, my father"* (2 Kings 2:12). Elisha was willing to commit faithfully to this "father" type mentoring arrangement with Elijah. It was out of the closeness of that relationship that Elisha was able to catch all that Elijah had.

It was also through such a relationship that Moses was able to be mentored by his father-in-law Jethro. Jethro's fatherly concern was that unless Moses changed his leadership style he would wear himself out (c.f. Exodus 18:1-22). *"Moses listened to his father-in-law's advice and followed his suggestions"* (Exodus 18:24). The fact that Moses listened is an example of the one essential requirement for successful mentoring. Humility meant he was not too proud to accept advice. Allowing someone else to speak into your life, especially when adjustments are concerned, can be a challenge. The best advice I can give you as a ministry leader is don't be a "know it all." Be willing to listen to and act on wise counsel.

Mentoring does not always depend on closeness of relationship and can occur at different levels of contact. There are several great leaders in the C3 movement who have mentored me indirectly by what they demonstrate and present from a distance. However, the closer the relationship between the mentor and the one being mentored, the higher the degree of benefit.

If you have access to a good and godly mentor, respectfully make the best of that relationship. If you do, your ministry leadership will be strengthened and enhanced. You can only grow and learn to survive with this kind of support alongside you.

End Notes:

[1] John W. Kirkpatrick, *The Power of Mentoring.* Kingdom Ministries, Auckland, New Zealand, 2000, page 63.

[2] John W Kirkpatrick, op. cit., page 7.

Chapter Ten
The Bottom Line

One of the most subtle dangers we face doing the work of the ministry is seeing ourselves as being "spiritual" because of what we do. We may constantly pray and study the Word of God but that in itself does not maintain personal spiritual life. It depends entirely on how much of that prayer and study is towards your own spiritual development. It is too easy for our prayer and study to become ministry focused. Our prayer then becomes focused on the concerns of the church and for other people, and our study primarily for message preparation.

It is subtle, but the shift in focus means that ministry gains precedence over your own spirituality. The ministry itself becomes central to your purpose rather than your walk with Christ. The consequence is the progression to doing ministry through self-effort rather than through an empowering relationship with Christ. To build on any other foundation is a fatal flaw. Jesus likens this to building a house on sand instead of solid rock. When the floods and storms come the house will not be able to stand (c.f. Matthew 7:24-27). The one sustaining source for ministry is to draw from

Christ's power. His power is accessed when you learn to cultivate his presence, not just for ministry purposes but for yourself. You must maintain an up close and personal relationship with Christ.

If your spiritual life isn't maintained, you will eventually be unable to cope with the responsibility given to you. Jesus said that nothing (for Kingdom purposes) can be accomplished apart from him (John 15:8). Nothing is exactly right. All our efforts add up to zero if we work outside of his power and purpose. While we are co-workers with him in the building of the church, it is only his anointing with us that makes it grow.

You cannot impart what you do not have. If the regular refreshing of prayer and the Word for nourishment of the inner man and empowerment for ministry is not happening, spiritual dryness is inevitable. When you reach this place ministry becomes a fleshly striving and you are overcome. Faith, patience, strength and tenacity dissipate under the pressure. Vision is clouded, perspective is distorted and effectiveness is diminished. In this place, you are easy meat for a knockout blow from the enemy.

The bottom line for sustaining long term, fruitful ministry is for the ministry leader to maintain a close connection with Christ. There are no short cuts to this. It is a matter of building a consistent devotional life for personal spiritual transformation, renewal and empowerment. Church growth consultant John Finkelde suggests that every leader should "divert daily, withdraw weekly and abandon annually." How this works for you may be different from someone else. Whether you prefer a more structured or more spontaneous approach to this isn't the issue. Being close to God is.

Staying close

Psalm 37:34 [NIV] says, *"Wait for the Lord and keep his way."* The word "wait" is the Hebrew word *"qavah"* which means to *"bind together by twisting, gather or collect."* If you picture the idea of taking two pieces of string and twisting them together into one cord, you see clearly that waiting on God is never passive. You don't wait for the Lord like you wait for a bus. To wait on God is to actively pursue intimacy with him and to do whatever you need to do, to know that sense of connection.

The important thing in your pursuit is that you make it a priority to seek God for yourself even before you pursue him on behalf of others. This sounds selfish but it is vital. You cannot impart real life unless you are drawing from and are transformed by the source of life itself. Our prayers for self should in part follow the example of King David: *"Put me on trial Lord, and cross examine me, test my heart and motives"* (Psalm 26:2).

A regular heart check is essential for spiritual health. I have learned to be open to his gracious exposure of wrong attitudes and areas where adjustment is needed. I have learned to receive affirmation of his love for me and to surrender to his Spirit for inner renewal. I have learned to receive his grace for my mess-ups and wounds. When you can hear God say, "I love you" with all your weaknesses and inconsistencies; when you experience his power for change; then you can lead others knowing God loves them and can transform them in the same way. Leadership from the revelation of God's enduring love for you in Christ is the only secure foundation on which to build both life and ministry.

Hearing his voice

When we are close to God we are more able to hear his voice. There are so many distractions, so many things shouting for our attention in today's busy world. Staying tuned to God's voice can be a challenge. Yet hearing his voice for yourself and for your ministry is paramount. His voice gives vision and guidance. It not only reveals the promise of your inheritance, it sets the pathway towards it.

Death Valley is a desert valley in eastern California. It records the highest temperatures on earth. This seemingly barren landscape holds wonderful surprises of nature attracting many visitors. In July 2010 three women set off on in their car on a journey of exploration. They particularly wanted to check out the "Racetrack," a dry lake bed known for moving boulders leaving tracks on the very flat and cracked mud river bed. The signposts were unclear and reliance on a faulty GPS navigation system led them forever in circles until they were completely lost. The story ends well, however. A few days later they were found and rescued from a situation that has many times in Death Valley led to fatality. This scenario is symbolic of a potential hazard on our ministry journey. If we are not listening to the voice of God for direction we can miss the way and find ourselves wandering in circles of confusion and frustration. Worse still, we can miss the destination altogether if we are not completely reliant on his leading and instruction.

Having a heart inclination to hear his voice must go with the ability to recognize his voice. In my experience God does not generally shout so that his voice is heard. Quietness and being alone with God are absolute essentials. Pastor Stephen Furtick made this salient point in a powerful message from 1 Kings 19 at the C3 Global Conference "Presence" in 2013. At a time of ministry crisis,

Elijah desperately needed a word from God. As he waits for the Lord to speak and as the Lord passes by, a mighty wind hit the mountain, followed by an earthquake and then fire. The voice of the Lord, however, was not in these loud, powerful and explosive forces. His voice instead came in the gentle whisper that followed (I Kings 19:11-13). Why is God's voice in the whisper? God's voice is in the whisper because he wants us to draw close to him. Intimacy with Christ is the prerequisite for hearing his voice. Every ministry leader must learn to regularly shut out the noises of ministry distraction, find a quiet place with God, draw close, and hear from him.

Quiet moments of listening for God's voice are not confined to scheduling extended times of prayer and worship. Such precious moments of listening can be snatched from even the busiest of days. It is a matter of living with a constant "God awareness" and the ability to tune in spiritually to his voice anytime.

Resting in his power

Staying close and hearing his voice are the ways of cultivating an awareness of God's presence. With his presence comes his power. His power enables us to carry out the work we are called to do. Jesus said, *"I will build my church"* (Matthew 16:13). Psalm 127:1 says, *"Unless the Lord builds a house, the work of the builders is useless."* God calls us to share in this work of eternal value. Even so, the work we do doesn't actually build anything eternal by itself. It is only God's Spirit that can do that. So what is our role in the partnership?

Paul, speaking of his and Apollos' work for the Kingdom, said, *"Each of us did the work the Lord gave us. My job was to plant the seed in your hearts, and Apollos watered it, but it was God, not we, who made it grow"* (1 Corinthians 3:7). The analogy is clear for anyone who has ever had a home garden. The gardener carries out the practical work of cultivating the soil, planting the seed, and nurturing the plant. But another power makes it grow. No matter how much you might will a plant to grow, or try make it grow, you can't. You can only help provide the conditions in which growth takes place.

Many ministry leaders forget this basic principle and exhaust themselves trying to make growth happen by their own efforts. One of the most freeing things is to know that you are not responsible for growing the church. You are only responsible to do what God has asked you to do: to provide the opportunity for growth to occur. Those are the things God whispers to you in the quiet place as you stay close. When there is a sustained heart connection with Jesus, from that connection will flow both the pathway and the power for ministry fruitfulness. I need to remind myself of this profound truth constantly. If I don't, I can succumb to a misguided sense of responsibility which creates frustration in my spirit.

To know that it is God's power that builds brings a spiritual rest. We all understand the need for physical and emotional rest. But rest in the inner man is also essential. Again, Paul writes, *"For all who enter into God's rest shall find rest from their labors, just as God rested after creating the world"* (Hebrews 4:10). While this can be a reference to the eternal spiritual rest to come, it equally applies to spiritual rest now. It is the kind of rest that knows God is the one who does it. For example, when I pray for the sick I do not carry the burden for the healing. I simply obey God's word and pray, understanding that the healing itself is God's. I can't heal anyone. Only Jesus can. All I can do is pray! That is the obedient action I take. The results belong to him. I have learned to approach all ministry in this way. Hebrews 4:11 puts it this way: *" Let us do our best to enter that place of rest."*

Our real effort in ministry is to come to a real understanding that it is only the power of God's Word and his Holy Spirit that accomplishes his purposes. We are to do our best to cooperate with him in obedience and lean on him in humble dependence for the results. That's what it means to find rest even as you labor. It is a conscious letting go and letting God. Go on, do it now! Relax and breathe out a sigh of relief. Let go of all the internal pressure, all the striving to make it happen. Rest in his power. There is an inner calmness that comes from that revelation.

Remember, it is his church, not yours; his ministry, not yours. He will build it! Of course you must do what you are required to do but don't be fooled into thinking that it is all up to you. Paul reminds us, *"It is not that we think we can do anything of lasting value by ourselves. Our only power and success comes from God"* (2 Corinthians 3:5).

Made in the USA
Middletown, DE
19 February 2016